BORN · ~~LIVE~~ · DIE

love

A MEMOIR

BRETT A. BLAIR, PhD

Born-Love-Die
Copyright © 2023 Brett A. Blair, PhD

All rights reserved.

This book is dedicated to my dear late wife, Kim Hannigan Blair, who now resides comfortably in heaven. Kim was an amazing lady who taught me and so many others how to live an abundant life through her example. She showed us all how to love and live each moment fully.

Kim's beautiful smile will forever be etched in my heart's memory.
I love you, sweetheart.

CONTENTS

Foreword vii

Introduction ix

About writing xiii

Chapter 1: Flourish 1

Chapter 2: Anna 9

Chapter 3: Kim 22

Chapter 4: Let the Doctor be the Doctor 31

Chapter 5: Honor the Struggle 38

Chapter 6: Irony and the Academic 131

Chapter 7: Born – Live – Die 142

Chapter 8: Caregiving 149

Chapter 9: Faith 160

Chapter 10: Silence 166

Chapter 11: The Choice 170

About the Author 173

Acknowledgments 174

FOREWORD

One of the greatest joys of my life has been to serve Brett and Kim Blair as their Pastor and friend. They are two of the most faithful, generous, and loving people I have ever had the privilege to serve.

Within the pages of this remarkable book, Dr. Brett Blair gives an up close and personal look at the precious value of a life well lived. Not only do we see this jumping off every page as Brett shines a spotlight on the beautiful and brutal story of Kim's journey with ALS, but pay close attention to Brett's life, as well. Together, this power couple puts on full display what it looks like to live this one and only life with purpose, passion, joy, and a contagious love that will inspire us all.

I believe that some people teach us how to live, if we will take the time to closely observe their lives. Other people teach us how to die, if we get the privilege to observe their final days and months on planet Earth. And yet, there are still others, a much smaller group of people, who can and will teach us how to live **and** die, if we will only have eyes to see and ears to hear. Kimberly Hannigan Blair was one of those rare people who taught so many of us how to do both. For that, I am eternally grateful.

There is this great verse in the Bible that talks about that sacred moment when one breathes her/his last breath, and they pass from this world into the next. It says, *"Precious in the eyes of the Lord is the death of his saints."* (Psalm 116:15) Kim Blair was a saint in the truest sense of the word. No doubt Kim's struggle with ALS and her ensuing death was a difficult season for the Blairs and anyone who had the amazing opportunity to know and love her. However, as I kept saying to our entire community throughout this difficult season, whatever you do, don't miss this—we are getting a master's class not only in how to live, but how to die.

So, let me encourage you to drink deeply from this well. The last time I checked, the death rate was still hovering right around 100%. In a very real sense, this story relates to us all. Therefore, it behooves us to seriously consider how we are living these beautiful lives that have been so graciously given to us, and how we might exit this world in a way that brings faith, hope, and love to those who know us.

On the pages of this book, you will find some of the best-kept secrets to making your one and only life count. Let me warn you; it's raw. It's real. It's transparent. Brett is breathtakingly honest in the telling of their story. One thing is certain—if you will have the courage to dive deeply into this book—this story will change you as it has me and thousands of others who were blessed to know and love Kim. You will walk away from this story more fully understanding the fragility of life, and you will come out on the other side a better person for doing so…

Here's to Born, Love, Die…
Dr. Benji W. Kelley
Founding Pastor of NewHope Church

INTRODUCTION

L IFE IS SUCH A CURIOUS AND REMARKABLE JOURNEY. AS WE grow up, we think we have things figured out, so we go forth, hoping we are right. Some people have things all figured out and live better lives. For others, they seem stuck, sad, anxious, or some other version of not living their best lives. My life has generally been somewhere in between.

I have spent the last half of my adult life trying to figure things out. Through shifting careers (from engineer to corporate executive to search firm owner to executive coach), I think I'm now on the right path, doing work that best matches my passions and interests. After a divorce and a long period of caregiving for my mother, I was now in a strong and loving marriage with Kim. I was enjoying great health and loving my work. I completed my Ph.D. in psychology, became ICF-certified as a coach, had a full book of clients, served on several community boards, and was active with our church. Kim and I were enjoying travel and fun with family and friends and loving life in our new downtown skyrise apartment in Durham, North Carolina. Kim was crushing it in her new career in real estate. Our dreams and plans for the future were aligned. Life was great.

Until it wasn't. At 4 p.m. on April 29, 2020, Kim was diagnosed with amyotrophic lateral sclerosis (ALS), a terminal nervous system disease. Also known as Lou Gehrig's disease, ALS progressively results in complete paralysis, the inability to speak, eat, and breathe. It is 100 percent fatal.

Going from perfectly good health to learning that she had a terminal disease in one clinic visit was surreal for Kim. The world shifted—things changed forever. Kim and I immediately embarked on a beautiful and horrific journey. I was tested in ways I couldn't have predicted. Kim demonstrated courage, grace, love, and faith that were awesome to observe and experience as her husband and caregiver.

Kim died just over twelve months after her diagnosis. I was with her, full-time, every day of those twelve months. We both took a deep dive into a new reality. Going from living to dying is an overwhelming shift. But I saw Kim fully embrace and live every day while she was dying. She smiled every day. She was more concerned about other people than herself. She didn't want anyone to feel sorry for her because she didn't feel sorry for herself. She had complete faith in God and knew she was going to heaven. As the disease progressed, she lost the use of her hands, then her legs, then her speech, and then her ability to swallow. Together we figured things out, like how to communicate during the months when she could not talk and other ways to stay ahead of the racing clock of cascading disabilities.

During the year of ALS, I was changed. The changes were good, and I hope they are permanent. I was forged into a new version of myself. I think I am a better human now: more alive and loving and faithful and fearless than before. It is those changes that I want to share with you, the reader, in this book. I hope you can benefit from our shared experience and start making changes in your life without the need to go through such horror as dying or caregiving for a loved one dying from ALS.

Why the title, *Born – Love – Die*? Because I stared straight at the fact that Kim was going to die and then the recognition that we would all die. It is just a fact. Unnegotiable. Guaranteed. It is going to happen—to you and to everyone you know. The only question is when and where, and how. You and I have no control over how we are born or how we will die. What we have full control over, if we choose to use it, is how we experience the in-between, the part when we are alive. The title of this book was originally *Born – Live - Die*, and I hoped that reading this book would help you live a better life. But then it hit me. **Love is the answer.** Everybody "lives" between being born and dying. But too many people let the fear of death steal their joy of living. Others are on autopilot, letting complacency or boredom, or laziness quietly steal their finite number of days left. I realized, and Kim helped me learn that **love** is the answer.

Kim taught me many things during the year of ALS. She taught me not to fear death. She taught me to love all people. She taught me to find a deeper love of God. She demonstrated humble courage and grace, which was unbelievable. But most importantly, Kim taught me the power and bliss that come from living and loving each day, each moment, fully.

One day, Kim posted on Facebook, with her fingers barely working, *"Don't let worry about tomorrow ruin your today."*

Living life one day at a time was ultimately how I coped as Kim's husband and caregiver. I found incredible power and beauty in living my life that way. I promised myself that I would continue to live life one day at a time after she died. I've been pretty good at that in the past two years since her death, but I want to hold on to it and get even better. Sharing this idea is one way I can lock in this philosophy into my own life and, at the same time, offer some practical advice to you as well.

I thank you for reading this book. If you are living with a terminal disease, I feel for you, and I hope these pages provide some solace. If you are caring for a loved one facing a terminal illness, I know this book can give practical advice and help you minimize your suffering. For others, I hope you shift into a new awareness of your life as one of "Born-Love-Die." I hope you will start living with more intention, more joy, more love, and less fear and start tapping into the power of being uniquely present in each precious moment of your only life here on Earth.

ABOUT WRITING.

I'D BEEN MENTALLY WRESTLING WITH THE IDEA OF GETTING started on this book for many months. I knew it was maybe the most important thing I'd ever do, write, or contribute to the world. I had such strong feelings about what happened, and I felt compelled to write them down, share them, and hopefully help others in doing so.

I woke up one morning with a clear image, a feeling, of what writing this book would be like. I saw a large, challenging jigsaw puzzle. When her hands worked, and even when they barely worked, Kim and I spent countless hours putting together jigsaw puzzles. We never did that before, when she was healthy, because she was too busy. I didn't do it either—I was way too busy. The busyness stopped, so we did puzzles.

On Facebook, we'd post photos of the puzzles we'd completed. As a result, friends sent us more puzzles. Some were super difficult. Some were easier. We both liked doing the easier ones. Writing this book and facing memories of such a sad, happy, complicated, and intimate time reminded me of working on a challenging jigsaw puzzle—a puzzle made of fragmented memories, feelings, and thoughts.

Once you've bought the puzzle, the first step is to dump the pieces on a table—a table big enough to hold the completed puzzle. You turn all of the pieces up so you can see the image on each one. Then you try to find all of the pieces that are flat on one side, as these will become the edges of the image. You group these pieces by color or pattern and match pieces that fit together to complete the borders. This is the easy part, the fun part. The hard part is staring, for hours and hours and hours, at the leftover pieces, studying the shapes and the colors and the patterns, and then worrying at the picture on the box while painstakingly trying to fit the pieces with those already on the border. Sometimes you get stuck, and it looks like nothing fits at all, and you stare, try to relax, and observe, and eventually, almost instinctively, you see a pairing and put it where it belongs. Sometimes you think, or are sure, that there is a missing piece. And then, IT APPEARS. Voilà. You just didn't see it.

As I wrote this book, it felt like I was dumping the memories of my life with Kim and the year of ALS, out of the jumbled box of my recollections, onto the table of this book's blank sheets of paper. Instead of puzzle pieces, I was now using my laptop and its keyboard, with my perfectly working fingers and my jumbled thoughts, in a desperate attempt to put together this puzzle of memories into a book, my book, called "Born – Love – Die."

Here we go.

> Found on my iPhone notepad. Dated October 2, 2017.
> A love story….
> Once upon a time,
> a boy met a girl.
> His name was Brett.
> Her name was Kim.
> When they met,
> sparks happened.
> They liked each other.
> They loved each other.
> They married.
> They were crazy in love,
> super happy
> for the rest of their lives.
> The end.

BORN · LOVE · DIE

Chapter 1

♡

FLOURISH

TWO THOUSAND PEOPLE OF ALL AGES, SIZES, AND COLORS ARE jumping and dancing to *Club Can't Handle Me* by Flo Rida. To someone from the outside, this would look ridiculous. The music is so loud, but the excitement and adrenaline are equally loud, creating a strange sense of peace and harmony. I look over to Kim and see her big, beautiful smile as she, too, is jumping to the music. She doesn't know that I'm looking at her. I have a moment. I have a moment of pure connection, gratitude, and love for this amazing woman. I'm still in awe that she chose me so many years before, and we are enjoying such a wonderful marriage.

Here we are, in San Diego. We're with eight of our best friends at Brendon Burchard's High-Performance Experience (HPX). I've been to Brendon's "Certified High-Performance Coaching" training and certification programs twice, and each time, I've been given ten free tickets to give to friends for the next HPX event. I've never been to a Tony Robbins event, but I think that Brendon's programs are similar, and they are transformative! Three full days of training, inspiration, guest speakers, and loud dance music during the breaks. It is frigging awesome.

It's February 2020, but the weather in San Diego feels like spring. We are having a blast with our friends, Josh and Mindy from Reno, Vanessa, and Brent from Wisconsin, Pam from Tucson, Jennifer from Phoenix, and Tiffany and Nicole from North Carolina.

We've rented an awesome two-story modern house from Airbnb in the city, and when we're not at the conference, we're walking around San Diego, taking in the food and drinks and awesomeness of such an amazing place. Because Kim and I planned and coordinated this trip, we got to choose the best bedroom in the house. Ours was the large owner suite on the second floor, with a monster bathroom and shower and a deck looking out over the hills of San Diego.

It's the end of the first day of the conference. We're all back at the rental house, showering and getting ready for dinner. With a reservation in about twenty minutes, Kim is rushing. I see her come around the bend and down the big, wide, wooden flight of stairs. Two steps down, her right leg buckles, and she almost falls, catching herself with the railing. She and I had a glass of red wine earlier, but I didn't think she could be drunk.

Dinner is steak and lobster, with more red wine. The full group has a brilliant evening laughing and catching up on life. Walking home in the cool San Diego breeze and taking in the moist evening salt-water aroma, I get lost in conversation with Josh and Mindy, both fast walkers. I realize Kim is not with me, but is way behind, chatting with other ladies in our group who are walking much slower. That is so like Kim, to be selfless and accommodating to others. I know Kim is much more comfortable walking fast—like me.

Kim not only walked fast, but she was also a runner. That was one of the many traits I loved about her after we met via eHarmony in 2010. Only a year before, having divorced Carol on (ironically) September 11, 2009, I was living alone in the house we had owned before the divorce in Brighton, Michigan. I was running my executive search company, Sanford Rose Associates, and struggled badly with the melted-down economy during the Big Recession. General Motors and many of the automotive suppliers who were my recruiting company's customers had gone bankrupt. I had committed to lifetime alimony and had just cashed my life insurance policy to make payroll for my little company. When things couldn't get any worse, I got a call from my mom, Judy. Mom was in tears.

"I have terrible news," she said. "I just learned from my lung doctor that I have a lung disease. It's called pulmonary fibrosis."

"Okay," I said. "How bad is it?"

"They don't think I'll live till Christmas. The only chance I have is to get a lung transplant. They're recommending I go to Duke in Durham. I'm so scared," she cried.

"Mom," I said, "We'll work this out. I'll go with you. It will be okay. I love you."

I went with Mom to Durham for a week of tests and meetings with the lung transplant team—pulmonologists, the surgeon, a social worker, nurses, and physical therapists. On Friday of that week, we met with the chief surgeon. He told Mom she had pulmonary fibrosis and wouldn't live much longer without a transplant. He then went on to say, "Judy, you are too fat. You are too weak. If I did the surgery now, you would probably die on the table. If you can lose twenty to thirty pounds and get stronger, I may consider putting you on the waiting list."

I wanted to smack this guy right in the mouth. Mom sat there and cried.

We drove twelve hours to her home in Niceville, Florida.

Two weeks later, Mom received a letter from Duke Hospital inviting her to enter the lung transplant program. She would need to move to Durham, live within a thirty-minute drive from Duke Hospital, and have a full-time caregiver live with her. Duke recommended that the caregiver be a family member. Me.

In May of 2010, I moved to Durham with my mom. We rented a dingy, dark apartment in the shadows of the sprawling Duke Hospital campus. I took my mom to physical therapy four days a week and ran my recruiting company remotely from my laptop and cell phone in my tiny, rented apartment bedroom.

Bored, single, and lonely, I set up an account on eHarmony. My third date was with Kim. When I saw Kim's photo on eHarmony, I was instantly attracted. When I spoke with her on the phone, I couldn't wait to meet her. When I met her, I was mesmerized.

Kim and I immediately started a strong and growing dating relationship. Mom had a double lung transplant surgery procedure completed at Duke Hospital on July 30, 2010. Mom recovered and was strong enough to return home at the end of September, and she walked the beach in Destin, Florida, without oxygen, with two transplanted lungs, and with the gift of new life.

My third date with Kim was to her church, NewHope Church, in Durham. I loved the church, loved the pastor, and Kim witnessed my love for Christ. We soon moved in together in her little apartment in Cary, and then, when her lease was up, we rented a house in an older neighborhood in South Durham. We married on December 30, 2011, and bought our dream home in the Colvard Farms subdivision in the spring of 2013.

Kim loved her job at Blue Cross Blue Shield (BCBS) of North Carolina. She spent most of her tenure in marketing but was promoted to Director of Community Relations for the state of North Carolina. In this job, Kim traveled all over the state and got to know movers and shakers in nearly every region. She was invited to dozens of community events, and I was invited to many as her husband. What a lucky experience for us both.

I found my stride in running my Michigan-based recruiting company remotely and was coached by my mentor, Dr. Tom Hill, throughout the whole period. Tom and I would have a coaching call once per month, and I am so thankful for Tom in guiding me to a goal-directed and continuous improvement approach toward living my life. One of Dr. Hill's mantras is "One person, attracted to you because of whom you have become, or are becoming, can change your life forever." I know that I attracted Kim into my life because of the goals I had set and how I was living my life toward those goals. It was certainly not because I had money (I was broke), was good-looking, or any other obvious feature.

While my recruiting company was doing well, my passion for the business was waning. I started to learn about a thing called Positive Psychology and took a course in coaching. I then began coaching people informally at first and then more formally. I discovered that I loved coaching and that my interest in running a recruiting company was waning. I ultimately sold my Sanford Rose Associates recruiting firm to Courtney Grant Tobbe, one of the first employees hired in 2008. I'm so proud of Courtney as she continues to flourish in this business.

I completed two coaching certification programs with Brendon Burchard and then the professional coaching program at NC State University. After becoming certified with the International Coaching Federation, I founded my coaching business, Best Life Global, LLC.

As I started to gain experience coaching people, most of whom were entrepreneurs, I was soon asked to speak and conduct training programs and workshops. I created a non-profit organization called the Best Life Movement and ran three annual events in Research Triangle Park, North Carolina, called The Best Life Summit.

As my interest in Positive Psychology grew, I decided to pursue a master's degree in Applied Positive Psychology at the University of Pennsylvania. I shared this idea with Dr. Hill during one of our monthly coaching calls.

"Don't you already have a master's degree?" he asked.

"Yes," I replied.

"Then, why don't you get a Ph.D.?"

I had not even considered that. What a great idea. That's the power of coaching—asking good questions.

I then researched different Ph.D. programs and decided to pursue a Ph.D. in Industrial-Organizational Psychology offered at Capella University. I learned that this would be a five-year program. I also found out, even though I am an engineer and I could teach statistics in my sleep, that none of my previous college courses would count toward the credit hour requirements. I was required to take several statistics courses over again. Oh, well, such is life.

Kim and I loved our lives together, equally thriving in our careers, enjoying regular travel and entertainment, and having fun with family and friends. We loved our involvement with our church and led several small groups and church programs. We both enjoyed meeting and welcoming first-time visitors to the church. We loved volunteering at the Durham Rescue Mission, being part of two different Rotary Clubs, and both served on various non-profit boards.

And we both continued to love running.

When I first met Kim, we signed up to run a half marathon together. In one of our early training runs, after looking over at this beautiful woman running beside me on the American Tobacco Trail, I said, "You are a runner!"

"What did you expect?" she replied curiously. "I included that in my eHarmony profile."

"I know," I said. "But I've met so many other ladies who *said* they were runners, but I think all they did was run to the refrigerator."

Kim and I ran two half marathons together every year. We usually picked races in the area, like the Tobacco Road or the City of Oaks, or the Bull City races. One year we ran the Indy Mini in Indianapolis, and we also ran in Savannah, Wilmington, Kiawah Island, Destin, and the Bay to Breakers run in San Francisco. We were now training for the March 15, 2020, Tobacco Road Half Marathon.

We loved living in our house in Colvard Farms and enjoyed the close friendships made over the six years we had lived there. We enjoyed volunteering at the Durham Rescue Mission, serving on different non-profit boards, and soon I became president of the Research Triangle Park Rotary Club. Kim spent several years as the BCBS Director of Community Relations, which was a perfect job for someone as outgoing and social. She was invited to community events across the state every week. I gave Kim pre-authorization to say "yes" to any event where she could bring me as her date. From Boone to Wilmington, Kim and I traveled to the best events, met awesome people, and enriched our marriage as a result.

But some internal politics started to brew inside the company, making Kim uncomfortable to the point that she considered leaving. We discussed it, and given that Kim had always maintained a passion for real estate, she decided to pursue real estate as a career. I agreed with the idea. While working at BCBS, Kim secretly took the required real estate courses, passed the licensing exams, interviewed several Durham-based firms, and decided to hang her shingle with Hunter Rowe Real Estate. She then resigned from her job at BCBS and embarked on her entrepreneurial journey.

As Kim's real estate business took off, my coaching and consulting career also grew. I sold my recruiting business in Michigan and dedicated all my time to coaching and working on my Ph.D. Socially, Kim and I were blessed to be invited to event after event, parties, dinners out, and more fun in downtown Durham. One night, after driving home from dinner and a few drinks downtown, I shared that I was anxious about getting pulled over for drinking and driving one day. We'd taken an Uber several times, which was a little expensive. Kim shared, "Wouldn't it be cool if we lived downtown—maybe just rent for a couple of years?" I replied, "That would be awesome! Let's do it." This short conversation soon led to us renting an apartment on the ninth floor of the downtown Durham One City Center building. It took several months, but we finally rented our house in the suburbs. Our tenants wanted a two-year lease. We eventually agreed and turned our excitement to the next two years in the city.

We moved into our modern but tiny two-bedroom apartment on December 15, 2019. Living downtown was amazing. With our cars parked in the basement garage, we found that we could walk to almost everything we wanted to do. The Durham Performing Arts Center and the Durham Bulls baseball park were down the hill.

Just to the west was the sprawling Duke campus, and all around us sat dozens of restaurants, bars, coffee shops, and anything else one would like to investigate. The American Tobacco Trailhead began across the street from the ballpark and continued twenty-three miles south to Cary. We loved running together on this beautiful, tree-lined trail.

We decorated our tiny apartment for Christmas but didn't do much because we knew we'd spend most of our Christmas and New Year's holidays with her family. I loved Kim's mom and dad, sisters, husbands/partners, and kids. With my kids now grown, being around little ones during the holidays was fun. Kim was so busy with real estate by now that we had to schedule time together for fun. I helped her write hundreds of Christmas cards, to the point that her right hand was almost completely cramped. Kim certainly loved people!

We were looking forward to New Year's Eve. The wine bar on the first floor of our building, The Oak House, had promoted their New Year's Eve party, and we bought two tickets. With champagne, hors d'oeuvres, a live band, and dancing—Kim and I were excited to have plans that didn't include driving. At midnight, we kissed and shared how incredibly happy we were—to be in such an amazing marriage, but also to be in careers we loved, living in such an awesome place in a town we loved, and blessed to both be super healthy and surrounded with loving friends and family.

The year 2020. The next two months were a blur. Kim's real estate work flourished, and her pace grew faster. I was thankful I had so much homework on the Ph.D. program because it was a good distraction from her being gone so much. We talked about slowing down, but then the phone would ring, and Kim would be back on, doing her magic and helping people with every aspect of buying and selling a house. She loved her work. She loved helping people.

We were happy. We were exhausted. We were so looking forward to a vacation. We couldn't wait to go to San Diego.

Chapter 2

♡

ANNA

"Honor the struggle."

"Feel the joy."

We heard these mantras repeated over and over and over during our three days at the HPX event. We bought T-shirts and hoodies with these phrases. On the long flight home from San Diego, Kim and I shared our notes taken at the conference. We had already written goals for the new year, 2020, but were now rethinking some and sharpening others. Holding hands on the plane, Kim leaned over and put her head on my shoulder. She whispered, "I love you so much." I replied, "I love you, too, honey. Let's live our best lives."

Corona. One of my favorite beers, especially with lime. I kept hearing news about a thing called "coronavirus" and was at first confused, thinking it must be related to some contamination or some other problem with the beer. Then everyone started talking about this virus and referring to it as a possible pandemic. Kim and I just kept doing our thing—working, exercising, and enjoying Durham from our cozy sky apartment. We were training for the upcoming Tobacco Road Half Marathon, and with the weather getting colder and wetter outside, we started training more often on the treadmills in the swanky gym in our building. Running eight, nine, or ten miles on a treadmill can be a drag. But we both found that watching movies on Netflix on our iPads did the trick.

"Ouch!" she exclaimed. I looked over and saw Kim jump off of the treadmill.

"What happened?" I asked.

"I don't know, but it feels like maybe I pulled a muscle," Kim replied while rubbing her right leg. She left the gym and went back to the elevator and up to our apartment while I finished what was left of my scheduled training run.

My fifty-ninth birthday was on March 13, 2020. Lucky me, this was a Friday night. I had forever considered Friday the thirteenth a lucky day, never unlucky. For many years, I bragged to folks that I was born on Friday the thirteenth, which was why it was a lucky day. Then one day, for some reason that I can't remember, I Googled *Friday, March 13, 1961*, and guess what? It was a Monday, not a Friday! I couldn't believe it!

I called my mom. "What day of the week was I born?"

Her curious response was, "Honey, you were born on a Monday at around seven in the morning. Why?"

"I thought I was born on a Friday. That's why Friday the thirteenth is my lucky day!" I replied.

"Honey, where did you get that crazy idea? You were born on Monday," she said, and we continued to catch up.

Wow. I was dumbfounded at how I had somehow deceived myself to the point that my lie became my truth. It struck me how fallible our brains, or memories, can be. I wondered how many other things I was wrong about.

But it was now Friday the thirteenth, my birthday, and we would have a great night. We could now walk to whatever bar, restaurant, or club we wanted because we lived happily in downtown Durham. It was a great night but strange. Many of our favorite places were closed, and those that were open required a mask. We met Reed and Courtney at the rooftop bar of the

Durham Hotel to have drinks while watching the sunset over the Duke campus skyline. We then walked to eat at Dashi, a cool little place upstairs on East Chapel Hill Street, where we sat at the bar and had authentic Japanese ramen with fancy bourbon drinks. The place was dark, cozy, and more than half empty. The bartender, wearing a mask, shared that he was worried about the corona thing. Walking home after dinner, Kim and I bounced into the mayor of Durham on the sidewalk, waiting to cross the street. Kim knew the mayor from her previous time working at BCBS, and he commented on how crazy things were getting with the potential pandemic. He went on to say that it might get worse in the coming weeks.

Saturday morning, with a hangover, I went out on our balcony. Looking out over the city, the sky was gray, the air was still, and an eerie quiet hung over the streets below. No cars moving nor people walking. Back into the apartment, I opened Facebook on my iPhone over a cup of coffee. Oh my God. I read the news that a lockdown had been mandated for everything but "essential services" in the city. I couldn't believe it! The whole city shut down? So much for the excitement of living downtown. Excitement was replaced with fear. The news was soon 24/7 about this thing, the pandemic, coronavirus, COVID-19. I started obsessing with tracking cases on the Johns Hopkins Coronavirus Resource Center website. I looked out from our balcony at Durham Regional Hospital to the north, wondering when the emergency center would be overloaded and people dying on the street.

Over the prior year, I successfully transitioned about half of my coaching business to corporate clients. I was proud of this and thankful that this coaching work would be more sustainable, predictable, and long-running. I was wrong. From March 15 until the end of the month, I lost all of my corporate coaching work. Many companies were forced to shut down; others were fearful and cut costs wherever possible.

Kim's real estate business was also affected, as showing homes became at first prohibited by several of the local city and county governments and then required special care in masking, cleaning, and staging times for showings. Kim and I both shook our heads at how quickly these outside events interrupted our perfect, fun life of living downtown. The presidential election campaign was also heating up, with tension building as an already polarized public seemed to get more tribal and agitated every day. The upcoming Tobacco Road Half Marathon was canceled, with it twelve weeks of intense training down the drain.

So much for an awesome new decade. So much for 2020 being our best year yet. Kim and I both adjusted the best we knew how. She continued to get new real estate listings and modified her routine to accommodate all the new pandemic rules. I shifted more of my available time to my Ph.D. program and recognized the blessing of the shutdown and reduced coaching load as a gift of time to work on something more important—my studies.

Kim was frustrated with her right hand becoming increasingly stiff and weak, so she visited two doctors for their opinions. Tests were run but revealed nothing conclusive—perhaps early signs of arthritis. Kim also continued to have trouble with her right leg and noticed that she couldn't do jumping jacks. A visit to a sports-medicine physician led to concern that she may have a hip injury, but a subsequent X-ray revealed the right hip to be perfectly normal.

One unusually mild and crisp Saturday morning with the air smelling like dew, I asked Kim to walk down to the Durham Farmers' Market and grab sausage biscuits at Rise. We were walking much slower now because of her sore leg. I stopped to tie my shoe. Getting back up and now walking behind her, my stomach sank. I saw it. Her right leg dragged like someone with a disability. She wasn't aware. I didn't say anything.

Kim was referred to meet with a Duke neurologist. When she received the referral to the appointment, Kim forwarded the message to me. I couldn't believe it! She would be seeing my good friend, Dr. Jody Hawes. Jody and I had spent a year in coaching training at the NC State business coaching program. Jody and I had become good friends, and Kim had met her at two different parties over the prior year. What an awesome coincidence!

The appointment with Dr. Hawes was set for 3:00 p.m. on April 29 at the Duke Clinic. Kim drove there, parked, and limped as she walked the long hallway to the neurology clinic. I nervously went to a coaching meeting with Brent, a long-term client living in Wake Forest, and thought about Kim the entire time.

My cell phone rang. It was Kim.

"Hi, babe. How's it going?" I asked nervously.

"I don't know," she replied, "But Dr. Hawes asked where you were. I told her you were at work. She said that after I get my EMG test, she wants to sit down and meet with me. She said it would be good if you could also be here."

My stomach sank.

Kim said, "That doesn't sound good, does it?"

"I don't know. I'll be right there," I whispered.

Brent knew that I was worried about Kim. I told him what I heard, and he said, "Go."

I drove straight to the hospital, parked, and entered the lobby. Out of breath, I arrived at the neurology clinic reception area, and a nurse escorted me to the dimly lit EMG testing room. Kim was on the table, lying on her back. Among the beeps and buzzing of electronic equipment all around us, I witnessed the EMG test's final steps. Looking at Kim and then into the eyes of the physician conducting the test, I could tell, even behind his mask, the concern developing with each buzz and subsequent recording of results on the fancy monitor.

I helped Kim move off the exam table when the test was completed. We then slowly walked to a small office down the hall, sat, and held hands while waiting for Dr. Hawes.

The doctor soon came in and, behind her mask, said, "Hey, Brett, nice to see you."

Then, Dr. Hawes said to Kim, "I bet you can feel some changes happening in your body. Have you guys had a chance to jump onto Google and see what might be going on?"

Kim said, "Yes, we have. We're hoping it's a slipped disk or a pinched nerve. We're hoping it's not something terrible like MS or, God forbid, ALS."

"I'm sorry," Dr. Hawes said. "It is ALS. Let me give you both a few minutes." She left. We held each other—and cried.

Dr. Hawes returned a few minutes later and asked if we knew about ALS. Our answer was a quick and simultaneous: "Yes." Dr. Hawes then shared that she'd make several referrals, including to the Duke ALS Clinic. She said she would try to get Kim in to see Dr. Richard Bedlack at Duke, one of the country's best ALS researchers and clinicians. Dr. Hawes shared that there is much progress being made on ALS and that we should be hopeful.

Hopeful?

Kim and I looked at each other without words, but with our eyes, we shared a common thought, a common knowing. Hopeful was not it.

In silence but holding hands, I walked Kim to her car in the parking garage. Kissing her at the door, she got in and drove off. I walked to my car three levels up in the same garage and, with my mind racing, somehow drove home. I saw Kim still sitting in her car in the garage at the One City Center. She got out, dropped her purse, and we held each other and cried for several minutes. We rode the elevator to the ninth floor and walked a short distance to our apartment. We went in, walked to the balcony, and looked over the city. Both breathing in the moist spring air, we gazed at each other.

"I love you," I said to this beautiful woman.

"I love you, too," Kim replied.

"Brett," she said. "Anna. Anna cannot find out."

Ten years earlier......

Dating Kim has been such a gift! Since we met on eHarmony six weeks prior, our relationship has grown. Kim has an awesome job at BCBS. I'm doing my best to run my Detroit-based recruiting company remotely from Durham while doing what is necessary to help my mom recover from double lung transplant surgery at Duke. Kim and my mom are getting to know each other and seem to be getting along.

Kim introduced me to her sister, Sharon, and Bo, Sharon's husband, and Emily, their cute four-year-old daughter. I soon learn Sharon and Bo are on the alert to receive news of their second child, also adopted, to be born soon.

It's a warm Saturday in August. Mom was recovering quickly and well from her intricate lung surgery and was invited to spend the day with her friend from Texas, Norma, who now lived with her grown kids in nearby Cary. Lucky for me, Kim was invited that same day to a party with her coworkers at an outdoor community pool in Chapel Hill. I was invited to go with her. I am excited and nervous about meeting her boss and many work friends. I am also proud. I am proud to be with such a beautiful and intelligent woman and will not take that fact for granted.

At the party, we meet a few of Kim's co-workers as we walk in and set up our lounge chairs in a shaded spot near the pool's edge. I grab two beers, return to our spot, and Kim and I settle in, watching the happy action in front of us. Dozens of carefree faces, kids, and adults of all ages splash, laugh, and enjoy the bliss of being together on a summer Saturday in North Carolina.

Kim reaches over, and I reach back, holding her hand. A brief glance and warm eye contact, held a little longer than normal, confirm our growing attraction for each other. I feel it again—that familiar sense of intense gratitude and almost disbelief that this amazing lady is my girlfriend. I close my eyes and utter a private prayer of thanks for this perfect moment.

Back at the pool, I observe three couples, with the ladies on the shoulders of their male partners, shrieking with laughter as they attempt to knock each other off the guys' backs. I quickly remembered doing the same thing in a previous version of my life. My life had so many previous versions, and this was one of the good ones.

A young woman's head comes out of the pool, with her hands on the side and well-toned arms gracefully and confidently pulling herself up. Her black hair is slicked back, and I am taken by how pretty this young lady is. A flashback of Bo Derek coming out of the ocean on the beach in the movie *10* races across my mind. Finally, out of the pool, I am more taken. By the innocence on her face, I am sure she isn't at all aware. Her yellow bikini top is nearly transparent. The nipples on both breasts are in clear view. Standing ten feet in front of me, looking directly over my head, she reaches both arms back to squeeze the water out of her hair, rendering the bikini view even more in my face.

Kim squeezes my right hand. I look over and deservedly receive that look. That look that says, "Stop it." Kim has witnessed the same wardrobe malfunction with this mysterious young lady in yellow, and she knows that my man-eyes are getting a full treat that is not appropriate. I return Kim's silent look with my acknowledgment of embarrassment and "What do you expect?" from a guy in this situation.

Looking back at the scene unfolding in front of me, a tall, thin, muscular, and very handsome man runs up to the young woman, wraps a beach towel around her, and they quickly walk over to the other side of the pool.

"Stop that," Kim whispers as I watch the young couple walk away.

"I'm sorry," I say, "but did you see her bikini?"

"Of course," Kim replies.

"Do you know her?" I inquire.

"Yes, that's Anna. I think that's her husband. I work with Anna a lot. She's a good friend." Kim shares.

Shaking that image out of my head and returning my focus to Kim and the others around the pool, I return to the honorable guy I was when I first entered the party.

Later, in line for burgers, baked beans, macaroni and cheese, and all the other food typical of a Southern pool party, Kim introduces me to Anna. Anna, in turn, introduces us to her husband, Chris, and their cute three-year-old girl, Logan, who is tugging on Anna's wrapped beach towel, demanding watermelon. Over several games of ping-pong, we learn that Chris is a native of Durham, has a very successful marketing business, is a triathlete, and is training for his next Ironman. *Damn*, I think, *what a stud*. And how lucky he is. It seemed like everyone in the pool knew and liked him, he has a gorgeous young wife, a cute little girl, and the world at his fingertips. Oh, to be young again.

Driving back to Kim's apartment from the party, Kim shares how embarrassed Anna was from the yellow bikini episode. Anna had told Kim that she had just bought the swimsuit and obviously didn't know how see-through it was once wet. She asked Kim if she thought anyone noticed, and in typical Kim style, Kim said, "I don't think so."

The next few weeks are a blur. Mom goes to rehab every day at the Duke Center for Living, and she enjoys life with her new lungs and the freedom to breathe without oxygen tanks and lines. I enjoy dating Kim while figuring out how to best run my business remotely. I am pleased with how well my employees back in Michigan are doing with the company, with me gone. In many ways, the business is performing better without me there.

Mom gets healthy enough to be released from the Duke lung transplant program and to return to her place in Niceville, Florida. I drive her home to Florida and am there with my brother and his family to celebrate this event, which happens on Mom's birthday and includes a walk on the beach—without oxygen. Mom is so happy!

Back in Durham, I finished the month-to-month lease on the apartment I shared with my mother and casually moved in with Kim in her small but beautifully decorated apartment in Cary. Kim's two cats, Nigel and Napoleon, don't care for me, the intruder, interrupting their lives with their Kimmy. Before me, Kim slept with her bedroom door open, and both cats regularly had a play date on Kim's face during the middle of the night. I can't quite take the interruptions to my sleep, and Kim agrees that the cats won't be allowed in her bedroom. Neither Nigel nor Napoleon ever forgives me for that change in their routine.

Working from Kim's kitchen during the day, I always look forward to Kim returning home after her day at Blue Cross.

Kim comes in the door. We kiss. She seems subdued. I sense something is wrong.

"What's up?" I ask.

"I have the worst news."

Turning to me with a sadness I had not seen from Kim before, she shares, "Do you remember Anna, that girl in the yellow bikini at the pool party?"

Sheepishly I respond, "Uh... yeah, why?"

"Of course you do," Kim nods with that look. That look that says, without words, "I know that you can't get that image out of your mind." Looking away, she says, "Anna and I had coffee today. She told me that Chris, her husband, was just diagnosed with ALS."

My stomach sinks. I know a little about ALS, enough to know it sucks. I had done the Ice Bucket Challenge. I had read *Tuesdays with Morrie*. I was familiar with Stephen Hawking's struggle with ALS.

"And she's pregnant," Kim continues.

Time stops. Nothing makes sense. How can this beautiful lady, married to this stud of a young man with such a cute little girl, face such a horrific change of events? A disorienting wave of shame sweeps over me as I process this news. I recall how I had quietly coveted the happy, beautiful, youthful, on-top-of-the-world image I had created of Anna and Chris and their family and their perfect lives, to now hear, in a single sentence, in a single moment, that that entire story is shattered.

"Fuck," I say. "That's fucking terrible."

"I know," Kim replies as we hug each other tighter than ever before.

Over the next seven years, Kim, and I, along with many people in Durham, and others around the country, watch as Chris publicly shares his ALS journey. At first, he fought hard for a cure, for a life as usual. But the disease progressed, and he needed to stop his work. He moved from limping to using a cane, to a walker, to a regular wheelchair, to a power chair. He started slurring his words, and then he could not talk at all. He learned how to use a fancy computer gadget that let him speak using his eyes. Even with all of this, he created a non-profit organization called Inspire Media, with a mission to create a butterfly effect of good deeds in Durham and beyond. He was featured on the national news for hijacking a Krispy Kreme donut bus and giving away donuts around Durham.

Anna has her second child, keeps on working at Blue Cross, and steadfastly takes care of her husband. Over the seven years that Chris struggled with ALS, Kim and I babysat their cute girls several times. In classic Kim Blair style, she decides one night this coming weekend is a good time to babysit Anna's girls. She then calls Anna to share her plan. "Brett and I would like to babysit the girls. We're coming over, and you and Chris can go on a date. We'll be there either Thursday, Friday, or Saturday. Which works best for you?"

She doesn't give Anna a choice to say "No." That is so Kim. I see Chris up close with each trip to Anna and Chris's house. I see the disability taking over his young and perfectly healthy body. I see him gracefully struggle to move, to talk. And with every visit, I see his bright blue eyes, his big smile, and his courage. And with every visit, I see his beautiful wife, two giggling little girls tugging on her skirt, smiling, and talking and rushing around the house as if all is normal. Kim and I play with the kids in their front yard, do art projects, or bake something fun. And then, Anna and Chris return from their date, and Anna wheels him into their modified bedroom. Anna returns and thanks Kim and me with hugs before we drive home to our nice house, in our nice, perfectly healthy bodies, in our nice, perfectly perfect lives. I feel so guilty for taking my perfect little life for granted.

As the disease progresses, Chris' life gets more complicated. He has a feeding tube installed, and then later an artificial breathing machine. He has nursing support 24/7, with Anna taking over the caregiving role after she gets home from work. In the end, Chris is moved to Duke Hospital, where the breathing machine is turned off, and he dies. A private family service is held. Anna sells the house that she, Chris, and the girls had lived in, and moves to a new home in South Durham. She keeps on working at Blue Cross and enters her next phase as a single mom of two little girls—two little girls who have already endured so much pain and hardship. Over the years, Kim and I talk from time to time about how sad it was for Anna and Chris, and we are relieved knowing that Anna is now free of the intense caregiving journey and can get on with her life.

"I'm serious," Kim went on. "Anna can't find out. She doesn't deserve to go through that again."

Kim.

That was just like Kim. To think more about other people than herself.

Anna.

From a cute girl in a bikini to a steadfast pillar of strength as a wife, mom, and caregiver.

And soon to be my lifeline. My lifeline of knowing and understanding and support and hope on this journey.

Chapter 3

♡

KIM

Born September 10, 1969, in Washington, D.C., little Kimberly Hannigan rushed out of her mother's womb with a smile—a smile that would be her unique trademark for her much too-short life. Those who knew Kim well said that she had a certain kind of spirit, a spark like that of an angel. Kim was always a unique little girl and young woman, and a mature adult, but her uniqueness was amplified during her journey with ALS. I saw it. I was amazed by it. I don't know how to explain it. I'm sure it was a combination of nature and nurture. Whatever it was, it worked and created one of the most loving humans on earth. She loved everyone, and she loved God.

Kim was born to Elsie and Larry, a young suburban couple of Irish descent. She was the youngest of three girls, each only eighteen months apart. Eldest was Sharon, next was Marsha, and then there was Kimmie. Larry commuted to work from Olney, the small Maryland town that the family lived in, to Washington, D.C. He carpooled with others taking the same route and was always the most talkative—he never met a stranger. Larry worked at the U.S. Government Printing Office and was friends with folks of all colors, accents, and political persuasions. Elise, a devout Catholic, worked first as a secretary and then was busy at home as a mother after hosting three little girls onto the scene.

As a little girl, Kim was always busy, smiling, and up to mischief.

Larry loved watching Kim play soccer. The Hannigan house in Olney was the favorite on the street, with boys and girls convening there after school and on weekends. Christmas Eve at the Hannigan house was an epic event for the vast group of friends the three Hannigan girls had collected over the years, with teenagers converging from across the county and staying up until daylight.

In high school, Kim was fit, cute, smart, hard-working, and everyone's friend. She worked at a local ice cream shop and was also a waitress. She attended the University of Maryland but got lost in the massive student body. She then transferred to a much smaller and more manageable Towson University, where she thrived. Working the summers as a waitress at a restaurant in Ocean City, Kim met and fell in love with Dan. Kim went on to graduate with a marketing degree from Towson. Dan, always charming and easy to be with, worked as a salesperson for a contact lens company. Dan was offered a promotion if he chose to move to Jacksonville, Florida. Kim decided to move with him, and she soon found a job with Blue Cross Blue Shield of Florida, working in the marketing department. Kim and Dan married and bought a cute house two blocks off the beach in Jacksonville.

When Kim met Dan, she soon learned he struggled with sadness and mood swings. Dan had lost his little sister in a house fire when he was a young boy, and his grieving parents divorced soon after the tragic event. Scars from this memory plagued Dan throughout his childhood and into his young adult years. Heavy drinking became a coping mechanism. Therapy and medication helped Dan to traverse some of the darkest episodes of depression, but life for the young newlyweds was constantly interrupted and strained by Dan's depression and drinking. Kim compulsively checked on Dan, encouraged him, and planned things to help him be happier and healthier.

Although Kim and Dan were married in the Catholic Church, Dan soon found that he didn't enjoy attending Catholic services. In classic Kim style, she agreed to look for another church that they both could enjoy. Landing at a nearby non-denominational contemporary Christian church, Dan and Kim found new friends and deepened their faith. Kim joined a life group and enjoyed the growth that she experienced in her relationship with God.

Dan struggled at work and eventually lost his sales position. He began applying for and interviewing for new jobs. Months went by without success. During this time, Kim's career flourished, with exciting projects and interesting things to learn about marketing. Kim enjoyed early morning runs with several ladies from the office and trained rigorously for an upcoming half marathon. Feeling stressed and exhausted by the challenges of Dan's mood swings, Kim joined Al-Anon. She learned she was co-dependent and began working with a therapist to improve on that aspect. Kim also found support from her church life group as she opened up about the challenges at home. And Kim prayed. She prayed that Dan would find a way to quit drinking so much. She prayed that he would find a job. She prayed that he would conquer the depression and be happy.

"Hi, honey," Dan said as Kim answered her cell phone. "How's it going?"

"I'm good," Kim replied. "I'm on my way home now. Can I get you anything?"

It was Friday night. Dan and Kim had no plans for the weekend. The weather forecast was good, so they'd probably walk to the beach with their lounge chairs and a cooler, drink beer, and play frisbee. They loved living close to the beach and looked forward to lazy, hot summer weekends.

"No, I'm fine. See you soon," Dan answered as he hung up the phone.

Driving a little faster than normal, Kim felt annoyed and uneasy by Dan's abrupt ending of the call. She pulled into the gravel drive and walked into the back door of their recently remodeled, comfy home.

The smell was overwhelming. A scent she instantly recalled from their recent trip to the shooting range. Gunpowder.

"Dan?" she cried out as she rounded the corner into the small office they had recently decorated.

Dan's head was down on the desk. He was breathing rapidly but shallowly. Blood flowed off the desk and onto the rug. A pistol lay on the floor.

Kim instinctively dialed 911 and calmly told the dispatcher that her husband had shot himself, provided the address, and waited for the police and ambulance to arrive. In shock, Kim rubbed Dan's back until the team came. As a police officer asked Kim questions, the paramedics placed Dan on a stretcher and into the waiting ambulance.

Dan died the following morning. A handwritten note to Kim was found on the desk. A ladder was found under a displaced ceiling tile in the guest room. The police surmised that this was where Dan had kept the gun. Kim and Dan never owned guns. A routine investigation found that Dan had legally purchased the pistol the week before.

Over the coming hours, days, weeks, and months, Kim's mind tugged between finding the key to what she could have done to prevent Dan from shooting himself—to reminding herself what she had been taught in Al-Anon and her therapy sessions, that suicide is an irrational act conducted by a person with an irrational mind.

"There is no rational explanation for an irrational act," she often reminded herself.

Held up by her faith, prayer and surrounding herself with church and work friends, Kim set about moving forward, one step at a time—one day at a time. A young widow, far away from her childhood home and friends, Kim was determined to move forward.

Using some of the life insurance money, Kim bought a townhouse, also close to the beach. She rented out the house Dan died in and avoided driving by it as much as possible. She focused on work and church, and exercise. Ongoing therapy was helpful; she felt ready to date again after two years.

Jacksonville Beach is a small town. When Kim and Dan lived there together, they made many friends in the area. As Kim attempted the dating scene, she found she could not escape the stigma of being a young widow. No one invited her out after work or to gatherings, and many of her friends disappeared. She soon faced another challenge—layoff. Blue Cross Blue Shield of Florida had initiated a massive cost-cutting initiative, and Kim's job was a victim. She soon found herself looking for work.

A few years before Dan's death, Emily, Kim's niece, was brought into the family. Kim loved being Emily's aunt and couldn't get over how quickly Emily grew in her first two years. Her parents, Sharon and Bo, lived in Cary, North Carolina. Kim traveled there as often as possible, mainly to spend time with her cute little niece. With the Jacksonville job hunt dragging on and deeply missing being part of her fast-growing niece's life, Kim decided to move to North Carolina. Kim applied for an opening in the marketing department at Blue Cross Blue Shield of North Carolina. She was soon interviewed, offered, and accepted the position with her new office in Chapel Hill, North Carolina. At forty-one years old, widowed, and knowing no one except for her sister and family, Kim courageously loaded up a U-Haul and relocated to a new town and a new life.

She lived with Sharon and Bo for a few weeks while acclimating to the area and soon rented an apartment midway between Sharon's house and the BCBS offices. She adopted two kittens—Napoleon and Nigel. After some church shopping, she found a fast-growing non-denominational church in Durham that she loved. Quickly involved with activities at work and volunteering at church, Kim was soon surrounded and lifted by a whole set of new friends. Thankfully, Amy, one of her new friends at NewHope Church, also single, encouraged Kim to try online dating. Kim reluctantly set up a profile on eHarmony. After several less-than-great dates, Kim and I met on the dating site. It was magic. It was love at first sight. Thank you, Amy!

Kim and I met in person on July 1, 2010. Two weeks later, Sharon and Bo adopted a second child, Tommy. Kim and I loved being around the growing Degnan family and regular travel to see my family in Colorado and Florida. We moved in together in her apartment at the end of October 2010. We rented a house together in the summer of 2011 and married on December 30, 2011. We bought our first house in 2013 and fell in love with the neighborhood and the neighbors.

Kim finished her MBA with honors, got promoted to Director of Community Relations at Blue Cross, and led several volunteer groups at NewHope Church. In her role at Blue Cross, Kim traveled regularly and became friends with interesting and important people across the state. A graduate of the prestigious "Leadership North Carolina" program, Kim was on the fast track at work to assume higher-level roles. As mentioned, I sold my Michigan-based recruiting company and focused on growing my executive coaching business. I decided to pursue my dream of attaining a Ph.D. in psychology. After being accepted into the five-year program, I soon found myself buried in homework. Kim, always the supportive wife, encouraged me every step of the way. I enjoyed being part of Kim's life and career, and we enjoyed being together in most things. We trained for and ran two half marathons together every year. We led a small group at church. I supported Kim; she supported me; we were both super independent, and our overlap was like magic. Life was good, and it was hard to imagine it being any better. I loved Kim in so many ways, but her infectious smile and positivity were at the top of the list of her attributes.

And then, there was integrity. Kim was honest to the core. In our eleven years of marriage, I can't remember a time when she lied or was dishonest. Integrity was so integral to her being. I must give her parents full credit for that, as I saw the same type of integrity on full display in their lives.

The door slammed as Kim walked in from the garage. I knew something was wrong, as she never slammed the door. Coming into the kitchen and tossing her backpack on the kitchen table, I was now sure that something deep was troubling her.

"Hi, babe. What's wrong?" I asked as she kicked off her shoes.

"I had a terrible day," she said. "I spent half of it in the HR office and then the chief counsel's office." Visibly shaken by what had happened earlier in the day, we held each other longer than usual. I could feel her sadness.

Kim was not personally in trouble. That thought did not cross my mind. But she was upset.

Over the next several weeks, Kim was asked to participate in an internal investigation of alleged wrongdoing by others in the company. Kim did what she was asked. She was saddened by what she learned had transpired.

Over dinner and a glass of red wine, Kim shared with me the outcome of the lengthy internal investigation. She shook her head in frustration, "I can't believe it. This makes me so sad."

"What are you going to do?" I asked, knowing the answer before I posed the question.

"I'm going to resign," she replied. "I don't see any other way."

"I know," I said.

"I think I'll go into real estate," she said, looking up with a smile and a spark in her eyes.

Kim secretly took the real estate courses and the state exams and picked a local firm, Hunter Rowe Real Estate, to be her brokerage. She then shocked her Blue Cross coworkers by announcing her resignation. No severance. No other job. Just courage, integrity, and confidence in her ability to figure things out.

Kim went on to become a top-producing agent in the next two years. Loving her work as an agent, Kim crushed it in the real estate profession. She would frustrate me by spending countless hours working with and helping first-time homebuyers instead of listing luxury homes or helping buyers with bigger budgets that would have made her much more money. Kim didn't care. She just wanted to help people. As a healthy Enneagram *Type Two*, "The Helper," Kim was perfectly created for the real estate world.

However, our marriage was becoming stressed. Stressed by the countless hours she worked, mostly on weekends. But I was supportive of her new career, proud of her success, and aware that Kim truly enjoyed being an entrepreneur where she could honor her integrity with every interaction and transaction. I was also thankful that I had so much Ph.D. homework and could keep myself occupied when she was busy with her clients.

After receiving the ALS diagnosis, it was sad to see Kim's new career end so quickly. She worked as much as possible for those first two months and was slow to tell her clients and coworkers. This was so Kim—always more concerned about other people's feelings and sad for them when they learned about her news. After shutting down her business and clearing out her office, Kim shifted her efforts to fundraising for ALS, staying in touch with family and friends, and spending time with me.

Spending time with me. Me spending time with her. That was the next chapter.

We were thankful that we both knew about ALS. We both saw the journey Anna, Chris, and those two adorable little girls had taken.

Dr. Jodi Hawes called, and Kim put her on speaker. "Hi, Kim. I have some good news. You'll be able to see Dr. Bedlack at the Duke ALS Clinic," Jodi said enthusiastically. "He's one of the best ALS doctors in the country," she continued. "He's doing several clinical trials right now, and I'm sure you'll be able to be part of at least one."

"Thanks so much!" Kim replied. "I look forward to meeting him."

"You and Brett will love him," Jodi continued. "I'll get back to you soon with more."

"OK. Thanks so much. We appreciate it!" Kim shared as she hung up the phone.

Looking back at me with both hope and knowing—a knowing that she was going to die, Kim took a deep breath. We sat, in silence, holding hands, looking away and then back into each other's eyes. We both knew. We both knew what lay ahead. Somehow, we both imagined a similar strategy—a strategy of how to best cope with the future. I didn't know if I could do it. I didn't know if I could manage to keep myself together, to smile, to be pleasant, to keep the faith. I didn't know.

At that moment, I knew she knew what she would do. And somehow, she did it. Her parents—they created the most amazing human. Her parents, and God, of course, deserve all the credit.

We looked at each other.

I decided then. I think she did as well, but we never talked about it. I chose not to go down the rabbit hole of denial, of seeking multiple opinions, of searching for alternative medicines or therapies or ways to stop or cure ALS. I decided to let the doctor be the doctor. I was happy to hear that Kim would be seeing one of the best ALS doctors in the country. But I also knew that no one survives ALS. And I knew Kim didn't want to live a long, suffering life in a paralyzed state.

I decided—let the doctor be the doctor, and let's live each day left to the fullest.

Chapter 4

♡

LET THE DOCTOR BE THE DOCTOR

WHAT DO YOU DO WHEN YOU FIND OUT THE LOVE OF YOUR life is going to die? I wasn't prepared to hear this question, but I think I somehow found the right answer. Or at least the right solution for us—for me and for Kim. Somehow, we were aligned in our reaction to such shitty news. We agreed to focus on the good and to do our best with the cards that were dealt. That meant to live each day fully, with joy, and try to see the best in each and every day.

Since we both already knew so much about ALS, we knew that Kim would die. We also both knew that she would become more and more and more paralyzed over time. It was almost unbearable to think about the journey that lay ahead. It was much better to focus on the day at hand, one day at a time.

When Dr. Jodi Hawes, stoically yet full of obvious love, care, and emotion, shared the ALS diagnosis, she immediately injected some hope (or tried to inject hope) by telling Kim and me about this great doctor over at the Duke ALS Clinic. His name was Dr. Richard Bedlack, and Jodi beamed as she shared her memories of being mentored by Dr. Bedlack during her prior years in medical school and residency. Dr. Bedlack even tried recruiting Jodi to work for him at the ALS Clinic. Jodi shared that Dr. Bedlack is leading the way in research for a cure for ALS and that several promising new drugs and therapies were being studied. Jodi told us that Dr. Bedlack is such a prominent ALS clinician that his waiting list is many months—maybe up to a year. Given her unique connections, Jodi shared that she would try to find a way to get Kim into the ALS Clinic soon. Jodi also explained how important it would be for Kim to get physical therapy, occupational therapy, speech therapy, and at some point, pulmonary therapy. Jodi asked if Kim had a cane or a walking stick. We looked at each other, eyes jointly processing the timing, the abruptness, and the implications of such a simple question.

Kim turned back to Jodi and said, "No."

"How about some hiking poles? They are cool—super light and retractable. I got mine at REI and love them," Jodi went on, obviously trying to lighten the mood. Yet, how could this even be possible? As Kim and I sat in the doctor's office, holding hands, raptly attending to the words coming out of Jodi's mouth, we simultaneously scrambled to make sense of the new reality we both faced.

Kim's first visit to the Duke physical therapy clinic was the following Thursday. Kim's limp was already becoming more noticeable, and her right hand was stiffer and weaker. Her second PT visit was on May 12, thirteen days after her diagnosis. At the clinic, Kim nearly fell when trying to walk backward, and a stronger set of canes was suggested. Although Dr. Hawes was confident in her ALS diagnosis, an MRI was scheduled to rule out any potential ALS-mimicking diseases definitively. The MRI took place at a Duke facility on May 14. As part of the standard process for anyone admitted to the procedure, Kim was asked to sit in a wheelchair before being moved to the MRI machine down the hall. Kim could walk. Yes, she limped a bit, but she could walk. Why the wheelchair? As Kim sat down in it, she began to cry. Then she hunched over and began to sob. I also cried but tried to hide it, to hold it back. This disease was moving at such a fast pace, but Kim was not ready to sit in a wheelchair. We drove home from the MRI procedure in my car in silence.

On Friday, May 15, just over two weeks after the diagnosis, Kim received a phone call from Dr. Hawes. Seeing who was calling, Kim put the call on speaker and said, "Hello!"

"Hi, Kim," Dr. Hawes said. "How are you doing? I'm calling to check in. Have you been to PT yet?"

"Yes," Kim replied. "I've been to PT twice, and it went pretty well. They've asked me to use a cane or walking stick all the time so I don't fall. I feel pretty good."

"Well, I have more good news," Jodi continued. "I just talked to Dr. Bedlack, and he has a cancelation. He can see you on Monday. I know it's short notice, but what do you think?"

"Oh, my God!" Kim exclaimed. "That's awesome. Yes, we can be there."

After some more dialogue off-speaker, Kim said goodbye and turned to me. "We are so lucky," Kim said. "Jodi told me that Dr. Bedlack normally has a nine-month waiting list, and I get to see him on Monday!"

"Yes, we are, babe. Yes, we are," I replied, with real relief and underlying doubt. We hugged, holding it longer than normal.

Dr. Richard Bedlack. Who is this man? I went into researcher mode. Hello Google. Wow! I easily found out so much about him. He was a rockstar doctor in the unique world of ALS.

Richard Bedlack...

There was something about that name. I dug into the corners of my memories, and it hit me. Don Brown. My friend and former coworker Don had recently posted on Facebook about being in Durham and seeing an ALS doctor there. I wondered if Dr. Bedlack was seeing Don. And then I wondered if Chris Rosati, Anna's husband, was also a patient of Bedlack's.

That uncomfortable feeling hit me again. The one of guilt and shame for coveting someone else's perfect life, only to find out that I was tragically wrong. The same guilt and shame I felt after learning that Chris Rosati, in the prime of his life, was diagnosed with ALS.

Don Brown. Don and I worked together back in the 1990s

at AFL. Don was an engineer, had an MBA from Vanderbilt, was married with kids, was too good-looking, and rising fast in his career. I admired how he confidently maneuvered his way around in all settings with brilliance, patience, and relatability. After being laid off as part of restructuring the company, Don soon found himself in a much bigger position with a defense company based near Charleston, South Carolina. At this time, I was also newly operating my Detroit-based recruiting company, Sanford Rose Associates. Don and I stayed closely in touch through each of our life's chapters, and I soon learned that Don's new employer, Force Protection Industries (FPI), was in an aggressive growth phase and couldn't hire people fast enough. Bingo! A quick trip to Charleston was scheduled. Don and I spent several hours together, he gave me a thorough tour of their massive factory, and I was awarded several senior-level recruiting assignments. This was a blessing, and my little recruiting company stayed busy with FPI projects for several years.

A larger defense manufacturer acquired FPI, and as is usually the case, the leadership team was replaced. Don's job was eliminated (again), and he (again) quickly bounced back into an even bigger position with a bigger company. This time, near Baltimore, Don and his family immediately settled in and thrived in their new city. While there was no opportunity for my recruiting firm to work with the global firm where Don now worked, he and I remained friends and would talk occasionally. With more money came more opportunities for Don. A bigger boat, more travel, a bigger house, living the dream.

And then I saw it. He posted on LinkedIn that he had retired. Fuck!!! He was younger than me and was already cashing out and living the retired life. I couldn't believe it. I then jumped onto Facebook, searched for Don's page, and saw a post of Don and his wife, tanned and smiling, with a caption stating that they're planning a month-long trip to the Holy Land. I had a couple of other colleagues from my early career who had made millions in stock options and other investments, and I was nowhere near that wealthy. I was jealous. I envied their lives. Now, I envied Don's life.

I sent him a text. *Hey, Don. I saw on LinkedIn that you're retired. That's awesome! Let's have a call and catch up!*

Later that afternoon, I received a text reply. *Hi, Brett. Hope all's well in Durham. Yes, I've retired. But, no, it's not awesome. It sucks. I have ALS.*

When would I learn not to covet someone else's perfect life, to discover that life is never perfect? And it started to settle over me. There were probably people who coveted Kim's perfect life. People who coveted our perfect marriage. People who were going to be shocked when they found out that Kim had ALS.

ALS. I was still a little shocked about those three letters. At times it didn't feel real.

Back to Dr. Richard Bedlack.

I wondered if Don was also a patient of Bedlack's. It had been a while since I had seen anything posted about Don and his ALS journey. From his Facebook posts, he was now in a wheelchair, but it looked like he was able to go on that trip to Israel before the disability made it too difficult to travel.

I emailed Don. *Hey, Don. I hope you are doing well. I've been following your journey on Facebook. It looks like the family is hanging in there. I have my bad news now. Kim was just diagnosed with ALS. She'll be seeing a doctor at Duke on Monday. His name is Richard Bedlack. I'm curious if you've heard of him. I'm praying for you, buddy. Thanks!*

Ten minutes later, I received an email response. *Hi, Brett. Good to hear from you, but I'm so sorry to hear about Kim. I'm writing to you with my eyes. My hands and my voice are gone, but I can use EyeGaze to communicate and play with Excel sheets. You know, I'm an engineer. Retired, but still and always an engineer. Yes, I know Richard Bedlack. He's the best. He's been my doctor since the beginning of my ALS journey. You'll like him. I'm praying for you guys.*

Wow. So much to process, to absorb. Using his eyes to communicate? Praying for us?

Back to Google. Yes, Richard Bedlack was Chris Rosati's doctor. That was easy to verify. Both Chris and Dr. Bedlack were sort of famous in Durham, so finding news articles about them took little effort.

Dr. Bedlack grew up in a small town in central Connecticut and attended college at UConn. With an MD and a Ph.D. in neuroscience, Bedlack completed his medicine internship, neurology residency, and fellowship at Duke. He also completed a master's degree in clinical research science. At Duke, he is an associate professor of medicine/neurology, chief of neurology at the Durham Veterans Affairs Medical Center, and the director of the Duke ALS Clinic.

While Dr. Bedlack is an absolute genius, what makes him most unique is his drive to find a cure for ALS and the unique way he interacts with and serves his "Patients with ALS" (PALS). Unlike most physicians who wear a white lab coat while at work, Dr. Bedlack wears outlandish, unusual, curiosity-provoking clothes to the clinic. He does this to lighten the mood and lift the spirits of the PALS and his staff.

Kim and I saw Dr. Bedlack and his staff only five times in person and one time on Zoom during our year of ALS. Each clinic visit included time with a nurse, a physical therapist, an occupational therapist, a speech therapist, a pulmonary specialist, a nutritionist, a social worker, and of course, Dr. Bedlack. These visits would take two to three hours and included blood tests, muscle tests, breathing tests, speech and swallowing evaluations, and time with the famous doctor.

We learned early on that Dr. Bedlack was both a clinical physician and a researcher in his role at the ALS Clinic. He lovingly provided medical care for his patients, lucky enough to call him their doctor. In addition to his amazing way of dressing, he had a cool swagger, funky glasses, a unique haircut, and an amazingly calm, empathic personality. Not knowing when Dr. Bedlack would walk into the examination room, Kim and I anxiously anticipated his arrival. He cracked me up as he carried a small leather black exam bag, as you'd see in an old movie with the doctor who made house calls in the country. Reaching into his bag, he'd pull out the little reflex hammer and gently tap the nerve points on Kim's legs and arms, intently observing her reflex responses. This seemed old-fashioned, but I learned to respect his routine. Another part of each exam was the dreaded ALSFR test. ALSFR is short for "ALS Functional Rating," a 48-point standardized scoring method to document a patient's ability to breathe, swallow, speak, and move. With each update, the ALSFR score worsens as the patient's disability takes over.

In addition to his work with ALS patients, Dr. Bedlack leads a ton of research. He has received research grants, participated in dozens of clinical trials, and has been published in academic journals more than 130 times. He is the past chair of the North American ALS Research Group and the creator of the international ALSUntangled program, which utilizes social networking to investigate alternative and off-label treatment options for patients with ALS. Most recently, Dr. Bedlack has led the ALS Reversal Project.

Kim loved Dr. Bedlack. So did I. I still do.

Imagine having a career where your life's mission is to find a cure for a disease that currently has no cure. Dr. Bedlack has been running the Duke ALS Clinic for twenty years and has seen over four thousand patients with ALS.

All of his ALS patients have died or almost certainly will die from ALS. Each of his ALS patients goes through a similar process of progressive disability. Every one of Dr. Bedlack's ALS patients receives his attention and care, and most feel hopeful from his unique touch. Most of Dr. Bedlack's patients with ALS participate in clinical trials and work with him in other ways to aid his research. ALS is such a strange disease, and Dr. Bedlack is such a unique man.

Thank you, Dr. Bedlack.

Chapter 5

♡

HONOR THE STRUGGLE

KIM HAS ALS.
 Fuck.
 I kept repeating this in my head. Well, not the "fuck" part, at least not always. But, damn, was this real? Yes, it was real. I was there. Dr. Hawes was certain. I had heard that it could take several months to diagnose ALS, that it is hard to diagnose, and that most people go through quite a journey to figure out what's wrong with them. In Kim's case, it came with one short clinic visit. Bam. The answer came. ALS. It was fucking ALS.

It's strange when your entire world shifts with one statement uttered from the mouth of another human. "You have ALS," Doctor Hawes said. Part of my brain immediately shifted into trying to make sense of this, to organize my thoughts, but to keep on breathing, to stay in control, to stay strong—strong for Kim, and strong for me. And Kim seemed to do the same thing. She shifted into strength and courage and grace. I watched her closely. It looked like she would sometimes drift into deep thought about the unknowable to come (and who wouldn't) and then shift into "doing." Into smiling and working and talking and loving other people.

This chapter is intended to share with you the up-close reality of living the year of ALS. It is written from my perspective—the husband, the lover, the caregiver. It is also written from as much as I can share of what I thought was Kim's perspective. It was hard, so hard.

But it was also beautiful, intimate, deeply moving, and life-changing. This will be a very long chapter, raw, sad, and ugly at times. It can be redundant and repeating, and relentless. ALS is raw and sad and ugly and redundant. And Kim was given this terrible disease, and I was given the assignment to drop everything else and take care of this beautiful lady, my wife.

ALS is weird in that, depending upon when you are diagnosed, you can go from being perfectly healthy (like Kim) to dead in a short amount of time or much longer. You just don't know. So, in the beginning, after Kim was diagnosed, she could do most of the things she did before, but just a little slower. She could drive, walk, and use both hands, and her speech was not affected at all. Her only troubles were a stiff and weak right hand and a sore right leg. She couldn't jump. She couldn't walk backward. She was working full-time and had a very active social life. The pandemic caused everyone to adapt, but Kim's abilities were pretty much the same as before. Until they weren't. Kim's version of ALS was a quiet, subtle, constantly hovering around monster, nibbling away at her physical capabilities. It did not affect her cognition or ability to control her bladder and bowels, but every other muscle or nerve-related part of her body was soon under siege.

As I write this dreaded chapter of this hard-to-write book, I rely mostly on my memory. But, thank God, I also have my journal. I've kept an old-fashioned, handwritten journal for many years, thanks to the advice from my coach, Dr. Tom Hill. I periodically journaled during the year of ALS. I'm so thankful for my journal, as it reveals aspects, especially the very sad ones, that my daytime human memory has forgotten or has hidden far away in a secret back closet of my brain.

I'm a Type Seven "Enthusiast" on the Enneagram personality assessment. An "Enthusiast" likes to chase shiny objects, stay happy and excited, and in pursuit of the future. An "Enthusiast" hates facing sad things and digging up painful memories. I thank my journal now and always for not deleting these sad memories.

Another thing that Dr. Hill taught me as my coach was to write down my goals daily. I've been using my iPhone's "Notes" app to do this. When Kim was diagnosed with ALS (April 29, 2020), I started numbering the "ALS Day" on my daily iPhone goal list. I still have the last entry of the 378 days that I did this—writing down my goals every day.

I'm crying as I recover this note. Here is what it says.

Goals w/ALS

Tuesday, May 11, 2021
ALS Day #378
Hospice Day #107

- Have supernatural peace
- Blanket this day with love
- Do this day without worry or hurry
- Serve well
- Grieve well
- Recover well
- Kim with nurse Tony
- Visit with Patrick
- Hospice visit / move Kim to Hock House
- Exercise
- Meditate
- Read Bible
- Prayer

Kim died. 8:30 p.m. Hock Family Pavilion

Sorry, I jumped ahead. Between April 29, 2020, and May 11, 2021, the time was a jumbled, tangled, blurred, surreal, hellish, intimate, and loving string of experiences: an intense struggle and an amazing gift of time and love. The majority of what I'll share comes directly from my handwritten journal. I'll also share verbatim words from Facebook posts and my iPhone notes. My first journal entry during the year of ALS was on July 4, 2020. A little over two months had transpired since Kim was diagnosed.

Kim was working hard as a real estate agent with Hunter Rowe. She had several deals in the pipeline and was adjusting to all the new and constantly changing protocols regarding listing, showing, and selling homes with the fear and confusion of the pandemic. Masking. Distancing. Sanitizing. In addition to doing her work, Kim carefully and thoughtfully shared the news of her diagnosis with her family and friends. Kim was so distressed by the responsibility to share her news—news that made others profoundly sad and shocked. This was so her—to be more concerned about others than for herself.

Dr. Bedlack and his team at the Duke ALS Clinic immediately put their full basket of support services into motion. We scheduled appointments for physical therapy, occupational therapy, and an MRI to confirm the diagnosis and rule out any other causes of the symptoms. By mid-May, Kim was steadily having more trouble walking and noticed her right hand was weakening. The first ALS Clinic was on May 19, and it was during this visit that we met the famous Dr. Bedlack and his support staff. Blood tests were taken, and a breathing test revealed Kim's lungs were in great shape. Good news. Kim was also taught how to use walking sticks and encouraged to keep her weight up. A foot-tap test was administered to see if she could drive safely, which she passed easily—more good news. We left the visit feeling pretty good, which was strange given that we both knew that a steady march toward total disability and death was imminent. It felt like zombie shadows grabbing at us around corners, but at the last moment, we escaped. I wanted to last as long as we could against the shadows—and fight to squeeze out their power in my mind.

We loved living in our apartment on the ninth floor of the downtown Durham "One City Center" building. Even with COVID and ever-progressing ALS, we still loved the vibe of downtown life and the incredible east-facing sunrise views from our wall-sized windows and balcony. But my love affair with city life soon ended.

Ear-piercing alarms throughout the rooms in our apartment shrieked at fifteen-second intervals. We woke with a jolt. I ran to the wall-sized window, raised the blinds, and looked outside. Fire trucks approached from the station down the street. Oh, shit! There must be a real fire. I flew into the hall and saw a group of our neighbors talking by the elevator.

"What's going on?" I inquired.

"Don't know, but there must be a fire. The elevators aren't working. We need to take the stairs."

Not smelling smoke at all, I entered back into our apartment. Kim was slowly putting on her sweatpants and a shirt. I told her that we'd need to go down the stairs.

"The stairs?" she said, looking at me with curiosity and fear. "Can you grab my sticks?"

I picked up her two new walking sticks from behind the coat rack, and we headed to the hallway. The shrieking fire alarm was even louder and sounded as if the intervals were quicker. We walked as fast as Kim could to the emergency stairs, and then slowly, using her walking sticks to steady her weakening gait, we headed down. With me in front and Kim's stronger left hand on my shoulder, we carefully navigated down each step of all nine floors. The fire alarm seemed louder and louder with each level of descent, and ultimately, we emerged onto the street-level sidewalk. Drenched in sweat and breathless, Kim and I sat on a nearby bench.

A cheerful neighbor lady approached us and shared that one of the neighbors on the eighth floor had a small kitchen fire, and the alarm was over. We could go back up. The elevators were now working.

Kim and I instinctively turned to each other. A tear dripped down the left side of her face. I leaned over and held her. We knew. We both knew. That was a close call. The shadows swept in closer.

Our fun in-the-sky-fancy apartment life couldn't last much longer. It was time for a new project—to find a house we'd move into for the remainder of the ALS journey.

When you get a terminal disease like ALS, people come out of the woodwork to give you all kinds of advice. Even though Kim and I agreed upfront to "let the doctor be the doctor," we were still vulnerable to some degree to listen to our friends' opinions. One of Kim's work friends strongly suggested acupuncture as a cure. I drove Kim to four acupuncture visits, and a very well-intentioned Chinese man did nothing except painfully poke Kim's scalp, neck, shoulders, back, and legs with needles, build up short-lived hope, and collect some money. One of my friends believed that an intense mind-body program would help. I watched a few videos but decided to return to the "let the doctor be the doctor" philosophy. And we could get lost in memories of folks who wanted to pray a miracle of healing. I'll reserve my comments until later in the book.

Our first road trip with ALS was a visit to Hilton Head, South Carolina, for a family vacation with Kim's folks, her two sisters, and their families. Kim's sister Sharon, who lived in nearby Cary, was a constant source of love and assistance from the beginning of Kim's illness. Sharon was my rock throughout the ALS journey, and I can't thank her enough. This visit to Hilton Head was the first time Kim's mom and dad and her other sister, Marsha, had a chance to see Kim in person with ALS. Kim's decline was obvious, and such pain and sadness were unavoidable in the faces of all who saw her for the first time. I had purchased a transport wheelchair and took it with us for this trip, as Kim could not walk from our hotel to the beachfront hotel next door where Kim's parents and sisters were staying. The shift from using a wheelchair for convenience and comfort to using it for necessity was happening. We both knew it but never put words to the shadows. We also both discovered that travel was hard and something we would not prioritize.

I forgot to journal for those first two months. However, I wrote down my goals daily and stayed super busy. Busy with my Ph.D. program, busy with my coaching business, and busy with managing the ever-shifting, changing, and accelerating challenges of living with and caring for someone with ALS.

And then, on July 4, I reached for my journal and started to make friends with it again. But, before I began to write in it, I dumped my thoughts into my iPhone notepad, using voice to text...

I know that if I journal it will be healthy for me to do so.

I'm trying this with voice-to-text on my earbuds sitting on the balcony watching the sun come up on this beautiful Saturday morning, 7/4/2020.

This is working pretty well, awesome actually. Just gives me a sense of how Kim can communicate if she's not able to use her fingers or her hands.

God is good. I'm connected to God in a way that I don't understand. I'm not my physical body. Kim is not her physical body. We are both unique, eternal, spiritual beings. I know I have some poetry bubbling around inside my head.

Stay present

Breathe

Don't rush

Be, don't do

Love God

Love Kim

It's ok to cry

Grow through this

Use meditation to connect to spirit—my spirit and Kim's spirit and God's spirit.

And later that same day, I wrote in my journal...

Saturday, July 4, 2020. Day 66 of the ALS journey.

Kim was diagnosed by Dr. Jodi Hawes at Duke Clinic at 4 p.m. on Wednesday, April 29.

Everything changed at that moment. Shock. Devastating sadness. Kim—amazingly calm, brave, strong. I love her completely. I've never experienced a love like this. It feels good to write it down. I'm lucky that my hands—my fingers still work. Kim's don't. That makes me sad. It's OK to be sad. I look forward to talking with my therapist on Tuesday, July 21.

How to be accepting, present, fully alive, and part of each moment left with Kim? I think that's my number one goal. What I've been saying as my goals are:

1. *Experience this with Kim until the end (not using the word "caregiver.")*
2. *Finish my Ph.D. fast and well*
3. *Take care of myself*
4. *Keep delivering great coaching to my current clients and new ones that come my way*

Sent a text to Clint Murray (coaching client) thanking him for recommending that I start writing a book, and that I have a new book in me.

Kim's right hand is becoming increasingly more paralyzed—very difficult to hold things or write/type.

I just set up the iPad with a touch stylus to see if it helps. She's slowly using her left hand. We'll see how it goes.

Challenge—ACCEPTANCE. Accept things as they are. Don't be frustrated by the things she cannot do. Or take on her frustrations. This is all part of the journey.

Take one day, one moment at a time.

Dug out the old fountain pen. Can't get it to refill.

Looks like Riluzole is not helping Kim. She had less energy / feeling worse today.

The daily challenge—how to stay present and make the best of each moment. It freaks me out how fast this disease has progressed. When I think about the past—the very recent past, and all the things we did/could do, it makes me sad. When I think about the future, it makes me sad.

As it often does, writing in my journal unleashed some deep thoughts.

Sunday, July 5, 2020. Day #67. From Journal.

Dear God,

Please intervene and make <u>TODAY</u> a good day.

Kim is dying. So am I. It is just that our timing is different. Please help me to remember that it is a blessing to be so completely in love and be able (forced) to shift to 100% focus on care for my loved one.

    Relax. Release. Accept. Be in spirit mode.

    No sense of time, space, stuff.

    Just love.

    Just presence.

    Just peace.

    Breathe.

    One day at a time. One step at a time.

    Awake at 4:45. Up just before 5:00. Napoleon is acting much older. I think he will die soon. I like my morning routine... without rushing at all. Kim won't be up until 8:30 or 9:00. I listen to the baby monitor to see if she wakes or needs help with going to the bathroom. I fear that she will fall and hurt herself.

    My routine—write ALS goals, take vitamins, make coffee, drink coffee with CBD, go out on the balcony, listen to the Bible app, listen to the Calm app, watch the sunrise, ponder it all. Take photos of the sunrise - maybe post to Facebook. Sweep the apartment while listening to a book on Audible.

    Now, listening to Jewel - Never Broken. Also—reading books about death and dying.

    Now reading The Five Intentions by Frank Ostaseski. He writes, "It is my belief that loving-kindness is the essential human quality most beneficial in the lives of those who are dying and their caregivers."

> *Mark and Gretchen have been in town since last Sunday. We've been getting together most nights for dinner and games.*
>
> *Mom is to have heart surgery on Wednesday. The risk of stroke is pretty high.*
>
> *Kim and I signed a contract to build a new home that will be ready in Nov/Dec—at the Courtyards of Southpoint. It is designed for wheelchair access. We hope that Teddy and Robin (our tenants at our home in Colvard Farms) will buy the old house.*
>
> *I'm getting great at cooking, and pretty good at Kim's hair and makeup. Eyeliner, mascara, blow drying hair, coloring her hair, and today I learned how to straighten her hair.*
>
> *Kim is doing her voice bank recordings. She's having a pretty good day.*

Wow! I could now see firsthand how this ALS disease was constantly changing. Even though we agreed to live life one day at a time, my private assignment was to live life one and a half days at a time. I was proud of my ability to stay a little ahead of Kim in making arrangements, buying gadgets, and learning new things—so we would be prepared when the next level or form of disability showed up. I was beating the shadows back—just barely.

Wednesday, July 8, 2020. ALS Day #70. From Journal.

> *Kim is noticing that her leg weakness is progressing. Wondering if working out more will help. I'm thinking that it won't.*

I'm trying to be better at accepting whatever shows up. I know where this is going—to Kim's eventual death—I don't want to let the horror of that reality steal the opportunity to find peace, joy, and LOVE, in each day, in each moment.

Today Mom is having arterial surgery @ Duke with Dr. Long. Praying that she has a successful surgery.

Yesterday Pastor Benji called me. He shared that he is pissed off about Kim's ALS. Me too!

I didn't write in my journal for the next 99 days. Not on purpose—I just got too busy or forgot or got lost in the fog of caregiving. Kim started her own private Facebook Page called *Living Each Day Fully*. Pastor Benji visited our apartment on July 10, which was beautiful and sad. Kim and I and our friends and family played cards, played Quirkle, ate and drank and laughed, and made the most of our time together. I bought a better wheelchair and enjoyed pushing Kim to local restaurants and the coffee shop/wine bar in our building, The Oak House. NewHope Church was closed because of COVID, so we watched church services online.

In mid-July, we spent four days with Kim's besties—Roger and Kelly, Jess, and Wulf—renting an awesome house nestled in the mountains near Asheville. We hired a private chef to cook a gourmet meal, toured a local brewery, played cards, made puzzles, drank wine, and laughed and cried. It was such a great time.

In mid-August, Kim was accepted into a 180-day clinical research trial with a drug called Clenbuterol. There was some evidence that Clenbuterol could increase muscle strength. Kim and I hoped the drug would help, but we knew it probably wouldn't. Later that month, Kim and I had a mini vacation at the house of an anonymous person who shared her waterfront home on the coast of North Carolina for folks with terminal diseases. What an amazing gift. During this trip, Kim organized her ALS fundraising campaign and walk and developed the "KimPossible and her Posse" brand for the campaign.

> *From Kim's Facebook page – August 21, 2020.*
>
> Curious what my typical day is like?
>
> For the next 24 hours, use only your non-dominant hand to brush your teeth, type, text, wash your face, wipe your bottom, lift items, eat, move the covers, get dressed.

> *From Kim's Facebook page – August 28, 2020*
>
> I read this good reminder this morning. I feel HIS presence all the time.
>
> "Fear not, for I am with you; be not dismayed, for I am your God; I will strengthen you, I will help you, I will uphold you with my righteous right hand." Isaiah 41:10

On September 12, over one hundred people came out on a rainy Saturday afternoon in the middle of the COVID epidemic to walk in downtown Durham to support Kim and a cure for ALS. Over $90,000 was raised, more than tripling the previous North Carolina record for ALS-centered fundraising. All of the money went to the ALS Foundation.

On September 17, we received a loaner motorized wheelchair. Called a powerchair, the machine not only allowed Kim to move around but also could recline and adjust in ways to make her more comfortable. Kim loved it.

In early October, Kim started receiving in-home visits from Duke physical therapists and occupational therapists. These visits primarily aimed to teach me how to perform "range of motion" exercises. These were various muscle and joint therapies to keep Kim as flexible and pain-free as possible as the disease progressed. The therapists also worked with Kim on adjusting and maintaining as much independence for daily tasks as the paralysis steadily took over. The therapists were fantastic, and became close friends. So good but so sad. With each visit, the therapists noticed Kim's rapid decline.

We also purchased a used Toyota Sienna van, modified for wheelchair access. The van had a ramp that extended out the passenger side sliding door, had no front passenger seat, and had a bracket that Kim's power chair would lock into for safety when driving. Our first visit to the Duke ALS Clinic, proudly arriving in our wheelchair van, was a nightmare. The sliding door and ramp would not work, leaving us stuck in the parking lot at the clinic. With Kim becoming more agitated, I called the dealership where I bought the van. My call was eventually routed to a technician who guided me through a complicated backup procedure to force the ramp to activate. Luckily, we were only twenty minutes late to Kim's appointment with Dr. Bedlack.

Okay...back to journaling. It's been exactly a hundred days since my last entry.

Thursday, October 15, 2020. From Journal.

It is 8:00 a.m.

A big, bold, beautiful sun is rising, and it feels good on my face.

I've stayed true/good with my morning routine over these past 100 days.

Wake up—usually between 5:00-5:30. Needing to go to the bathroom.

We now have an alarm clock that displays the time on the ceiling. Without my glasses, I can barely read it, but I can. Sometimes Kim hears me wake up and asks me to take her to the bathroom. Usually, she sleeps through it.

I turn on the baby monitor and can hear the frog sounds from the sound machine we always go to sleep on.

I write down my goals on the notepad on my iPhone. Most are repeats.

- Have supernatural peace
- Serve well
- Grieve well
- Recover well
- Blanket this day with love
- Meditate
- Read from the Bible
- Pray

I say a prayer first thing when I wake up. I try to connect to the spirit in me that is connected to God, and the spirit in Kim, where ALS is not a thing.

I get on the floor and say a more intentional prayer in the living room.

I pray for a miracle of healing, knowing that God CAN do that, but I don't expect it. If there is a miracle of healing, Kim would like it to return her to full health—not just prolong her current state of disability.

Then, I pray for both Kim and me to be at peace, feeling God's loving presence, and that we have a good day. I pray that Kim is not in pain, and that she can somehow be happy, or pleasant, or at peace.

I lay out the morning meds/supplements for Kim and me. I take mine. I put Kim's on a napkin and take them to her when she wakes up.

I listen to the Bible app—a devotional and then Bible verses.

I do 10 minutes of meditation (Daily Calm).

I listen to an audiobook "The Future of Humanity" while I sweep the apartment. Especially the kitty litter all over the bathroom floor.

Napoleon has been very difficult lately, and my nerves are wrecked over it. He is either asleep or mad—noisy—getting into things—a pain in the ass. Kim arranged for him to be adopted by an elderly lady in Durham. She'll pick Napoleon up tomorrow. It may be a sad day for Kim.

I had an unusual reprieve that evening, going out to dinner and drinks with my friends Reed and Sam. Amy Gillie came to our apartment and stayed with Kim to do "range of motion" exercises.

Friday, October 16. ALS Day #171. From Journal.

Today I feel hungover.

Betty Hill died last week—private family service tomorrow morning.

I'm sadder this morning than normal—maybe because I

don't feel good, the rainy weather, and Kim's growing disability is ever-present.

The speed of this disease is terrible, however, Kim doesn't want to live a long life like this, so in a way it may be better if it keeps moving fast.

We now have a Hoyer lift and sling. Waiting to be trained on how to use it by Drew (PT) and Hagar (OT). Both Drew and Hagar are great. Hagar is adorable.

My local support team:

- Dr. Bedlack
- Sharon
- Anna Rosati
- Amy Gillie
- Drew
- Hagar
- Lisa (Speech Therapist)
- Nadine Pennell
- Reed Frankel
- Brent Droege
- Patrick Harrell
- Sam Poley

My dissertation is turned in—to Liz Koman & two others on my doctoral committee. Waiting for feedback. Strange feeling—there's nothing I can do on the dissertation while I wait.

BORN·LOVE·DIE

> Material ←---------------------------→ Spiritual
> Born--------------------Live---------------------Die
> Chop Wood
> Spirit
> How long will this go on? When will she die? How will that happen? Can I do it? YES
> Get a glimpse of life after Kim passes.
> Kim's funeral. Big celebration.
> COVID
> Election
> Race Issues
> Breathe
> Be Mindful

Kim asked me, and I said, "Yes." I started reading books aloud to her when we went to bed at night. It became our favorite time of the day. In October, I read *Before We Were Yours* by Lisa Wingate and *The Book Woman of Troublesome Creek* by Kim Michelle Richardson.

In mid-October, I set up a Meal Train campaign on Facebook, and dozens of people signed up to bring meals or buy credits on GrubHub or DoorDash. Often, we'd have friends stay and eat with us. Other times, we'd prefer to eat alone. Kim almost always liked having at least a short visit with the friends who delivered the meals. I recognized that so many people wanted to help us, and they were quietly struggling in their ways without having any way to help. Allowing them to bring us food was a way I could bless them, letting them be a part of helping us, helping their beloved Kim.

Wednesday, October 21, 2020. ALS Day #176. Clenbuterol Day #68 (out of 180). From Journal.

Yesterday was the worst day yet. Kim was struggling to use the pole to get up and down to the toilet – stuck – mad – sad.

SCREAMING!

Then, I feel stuck, inadequate, like I can't cope.... like I'm not adequate for this role – this journey. I told her that. I asked her to quit screaming. She said that maybe she should be moved to an institution – a home for people like her. I told her NO! I want to take care of her until the end. I've already lost my wife, my friend, my lover. That person has already died. Now, I'm taking care of Kim. I love her dearly. I want to be able to cope better.

Today Sharon is coming to stay with Kim. I have four coaching meetings.

I ordered a commode/shower chair on Amazon today—will be delivered on Friday.

Next Tuesday Drew and Hagar will teach me, Sharon, and Kim how to use the Hoyer lift and sling. Maybe that will help with the stress of transfers. Still facing a decline in her left hand (feeding, brushing teeth, Kleenex, driving power chair) and speech.

Inch by inch

Day by day

Hour by hour

Born----------------------Live--------------------Die

It's just biology

Chopping wood

It's just a thing

Why not me?

SPIRIT

I feel like I'm Viktor Frankel in Man's Search for Meaning.

This is SO SAD. Taking care of my dying wife. She sleeps a lot. She is sad. She is uncomfortable. I get tired and my back hurts – but I feel like I can't complain. Who am I to complain when compared to what Kim is going through?

We had to cancel the dinner visit with Amy Baldwin last night.

I'm going to ask Josh & Mindy not to come. So many of Kim's friends want to visit – I need to prioritize that.

Need to prioritize getting Kim's rest, range of motion, food, hygiene, and love.

What matters:

o   Helping Kim
o   Finishing PhD
o   Taking care of myself
o   Coaching clients
o   Learning/growing/observing
o   Becoming more spiritual

It is a warm, foggy day.

It got up at 5 a.m.

The train is very loud.

I like not having Napoleon here anymore.

Will drive my BMW today!

Will go by the new house to check it out.

How to make meaning from this journey?

My goals:

- *Survive*
- *Be a pleasant and reliable caregiver for Kim*
- *Finish my PhD*
- *Be a good coach*
- *Stay healthy*
- *Observe*
- *Grow*
- *Be patient*
- *Be spiritual*
- *Plan my next chapter*

The sun is rising – to the right of the church steeple. God is good.

Stay connected to spirit all day long.

After Kim dies, there will be a funeral, and then what?

Alone

Where do I live? Stay in Durham? I think so.

What do I do? Money? Health?

One glorious day at a time.

Upcoming challenges for Kim

- o Hand paralysis
- o Speaking/typing/communicating
- o Swallowing

Breathing

Stay comfortable until death. This is my assignment – to help with this.

Ramp up help with Kim

Sharon, Amy Gillie, Nadine Pennell, Hagar OT, Drew PT, Duke Home Health Aid?

Born------------------------Live------------------------Die

How? It's a choice.

I choose to minimize suffering.

Suffering is mainly in my head.

Chop wood

It's just a thing

Why not me?

SPIRIT

Start with God

Stay with God

End with God

Nice walk/wheelchair ride to the Farmer's Market. Breakfast bagels from the Food Hall.

Kim is feeling better. Working on a puzzle.

Tonight, Caroline Delgross bringing dinner.

We spent countless hours building puzzles. We would post photos of the puzzles we made on Facebook, and then friends and family would send us more. It was a great distraction. I think Kim enjoyed doing something that challenged her mind but didn't challenge her physically. As her left hand started to fail her, she would tell me where to put the pieces.

I bought Kim a recumbent bike. There was a younger lady in Durham with ALS who was famous for staying in good shape for many years. She credited her success to exercise, so we thought we'd explore if riding a stationary bike would help Kim. When the bike was delivered, it came in a big cardboard box. The delivery man dropped it off in the front lobby of our building. I asked the guard if he would help me load it into the elevator and our apartment on the ninth floor. About this time, a lady barked at me for bringing a delivery through the residential lobby instead of through the rear garage and into the cargo elevator. I couldn't believe it. My wife was dying. I was trying everything I could do to help. Moving this bike up to our room would only take a few minutes. And this woman was yelling at me about which damn elevator I was using. My world started spinning, but I kept my mouth shut, and we went to our apartment.

Saturday, October 24, 2020. ALS Day #179. Clenbuterol Day #66. From Journal.

Up at 5:20.

Tiffany Cooper brought over lasagna and salad last night. She stayed and had dinner with us.

Yesterday I received and assembled a commode chair that we can use with the Hoyer lift.

This week Drew helped Kim get on and ride her new recumbent bike. That was awesome.

I'm making great progress on my dissertation. Waiting for feedback from Dr. McCaslin.

How to make meaning from this journey?

My goals:

Survive

Be a pleasant and reliable caregiver for Kim

Finish my PhD

Be a good coach

Stay healthy

Observe

Grow

Be patient

Be spiritual

Plan my next chapter

Sun is rising—to the right of the church steeple. God is good.

Stay connected to spirit all day long.

After Kim dies, there will be a funeral, and then what?

> *Alone*
>
> *Where do I live? Stay in Durham? I think so.*
>
> *What do I do?*
>
> *Money?*
>
> *Health?*
>
> *Family – Dana, Patrick, Mom, Dad*
>
> *Friends*
>
> *Dr. Brett Blair – what do I want to do with this*

One glorious day at a time.

Kim could still use her left fingers to type on her laptop. Slowly, but she could do it. She continued to upload photos and videos and write posts on her *Living Each Day Fully* Facebook page.

October 31, 2020. From Kim's Living Each Day Fully Facebook Page

Hey Gang. I just wanted to share that I am feeling so grateful!

Kind of crazy, right? Over the last few months, I have been showered with love. I am so thankful for all the cards, flowers, puzzles, texts, meals, and visits.

Brett Blair has been the best life partner! He is amazing in so many ways. I am richly blessed by his love and support.

And others have been coming to hang out with me to give him a break. I am so thankful for Sharon, Anna, Amy, and Nadine.

I know that it is God's grace and peace that helps me to say positive and full of joy.

The kindness of you all makes my heart smile. Thank you, thank you, thank you.

November 1, 2020. ALS Day #187. Clenbuterol Day #74. From Journal.

Terrible day! Maybe the worst yet.

After giving Kim a shower, dressing her, and then trying to transfer her from her bench to the power chair, she got stuck, and then uncontrollable laughter, and then crying.

I HATE IT when she does this.

But it is a side effect of the FUCKING ALS disease, so I need to get used to it.

I don't know how much longer I can cope when she does this.

Breathe....

This will pass...

One day at a time......

.... One hour at a time.

I hate it when Kim glares at me like that.

Born------------------Live------------------Die

It's just a thing

Why not me?

Chop wood.

SPIRIT

November 2, 2020. ALS Day #188. Clenbuterol Day #75. From Journal.

Born --------------------Live------------------Die

It's just a thing

Chop wood

Why not me?

SPIRIT

9:00 – Kim is not awake yet

Used shower chair to potty at 2 a.m.

Kim is getting very unstable in using the pole in the guest bath for the toilet.

I am afraid she is going to fall

Today Hagar is going to help get Kim into the hot tub up on the roof.

My goal: Be lovingly and cheerfully present all day as Kim's caregiver. All in. Today.

Working on:

- Final pieces of dissertation
    - Make final conference call presentation
- New wheelchair
- ALS speech-generating device

- Go to the new house – 11 a.m.
  - Pre-drywall meeting
- Talk to Anna about GoFundMe

Today –
- Eat better / less (stomach not good / weight gain)
- No alcohol tonight
- Kim – range of motion exercises
- Kim on the recumbent bike

With help from a friend of Kim's, we set up a GoFundMe page. We were blessed with thousands of dollars donated. We also received a new, permanent power chair from Stall's Medical. It fit Kim's body better, and she loved it!

Saturday, November 14. ALS Day #200. Clenbuterol Day #87. From Journal.

I'm sad, but I think I'm healthy. I'm OK. Kim is still asleep (9:13 a.m.).

Last night we had dinner and drinks up on the 28th floor with Jen & Steve Arnold.

Kim is having much more difficulty speaking. Clinic visit was on Tuesday 11/10 – to check on how her clinical trial is going. Not good.

Kim's ALS score – 23 (out of 48).

We go back for a clinic visit on 11/17, and will have an "augmentative communication evaluation" with Jill Marcus (Speech Therapist) and Kevin Caves (Rehab Engineer). I'm so looking forward to Kim being able to use the EyeGaze device for speaking and for using the internet. We will find out Kim's breathing score on Tuesday as well.

Even though I dread going to the ALS Clinic, I always feel better when we're there. I'm honored that Dr. Bedlack and his staff see ALS patients every day (each of whom will die), so they are not surprised or discouraged by what they see. At the visit on Tuesday, Kim told me that she traded eye contact with another lady who had ALS and was leaning way back in her power chair — appeared to be much further along than Kim.

I'm waiting for Kim to call out "Brettita." That's what she calls me when she wants me to come get her up. It's getting harder to transfer her (from bed to powerchair).

We've been using the toilet wheelchair in the mornings to take her to the potty. Still using the pole with raised toilet seat for bathroom the rest of the day. Who knows how much longer?

I'm NOT looking forward to using the Hoyer lift. I know Kim is not either.

Kim Born--------------------Live-----------------------Die

Brett Born--------------------Live----------------------Die

My assignment today

Chop Wood

It's just a thing

Why not me?

Why not Kim?

> SPIRIT
>
> Make today a GOOD day!

I found that I was journaling more and more, partially because it was so hard to behave, think, and live with joy, peace, and resilience. I was leaning on my daily journal as a trick to help me do this caregiving thing better.

Monday, November 16, 2020. ALS Day #202. Clenbuterol Day #89. From Journal.

Sun is rising. 6:57 a.m.

I woke up at 4:30. Up at 4:50. Slept poorly.

Kim is very sad/depressed.

She told me yesterday that she doesn't want to fight this anymore.

She pissed me off when she scolded me. Told me to count to ten — when I was trying to transfer her to the toilet. She started laughing uncontrollably and then peed on the power chair.

I'm doing all I can, and I hate it when it is not enough. I decided I needed to get more help. 4 hours every morning. 8-12? Need to get Kim to agree.

What would help do? Get Kim up, to the bathroom, dressed, brush her teeth, hair, breakfast. Range of motion exercises. Bathroom.

I am defending my dissertation on Friday at 3 p.m.

Ph.D. has been a five-year journey — started in December

2015. I already know there will be a big, empty feeling after I finish.

Dr. Brett Blair – I/O Psychologist

Brett Alan Blair, Ph.D.

What to do with this? Coach, teach, consult, research, write, real estate?

November 22, 2020. From Kim's Living Each Day Fully Facebook Page

Hope everyone is doing well and enjoying cooler weather. It's been a while since I've given an update, so here goes.

After recent visits to the ALS clinic, we learned the following:

The clinical trial has revealed no positive impact. We are 3 months into a six-month trial. I will continue to take the drug to see the trial through to the end.

The disease continues to progress at a quick rate, unfortunately. My functional rating score went to a 23 from 29 at my last visit. The evaluation primarily assesses my ability to do daily tasks independently.

My breathing evaluation revealed that I am entering the not-so-good range when it comes to my ability to cough and clear my throat if needed. In the range of 50 to 80 they start assessing if support is needed to breathe. I scored a 79. The next step, when needed, is a BiPAP machine at night.

On a positive note, I looked at tools to help me type and

speak with a computer using my eyes as the mouse. We will test two of the available options in more detail before selecting a tool. This will help me as speech is getting more difficult. Once purchased, my voice recording will be loaded into it. It will still sound like a robot, but with my voice.

Regarding other news, I have my electric wheelchair that was measured for me. It is amazing. We also ordered an adjustable bed so that I might be able to get better sleep. Lastly, we are looking at resources to get more support in the home, including transfers and range of motion exercises. It is a full-time job taking care of me.

Love you all. Hugs.

Monday, November 23, 2020. From Journal

4:09 p.m. Sitting at the window of the bar at the Oak House.

On Friday, 11/20, from 3-4 p.m., on Zoom video, I defended my dissertation. It went GREAT! All three on my committee pushed me to write journal articles and get peer-reviewed published. That was awesome to hear.

It was weird to get all the way to successfully defending my dissertation, after five years of effort, and having no celebration or recognition. Such is the situation in serving Kim through the ALS journey.

She is declining so very, very fast.

At the ALS Clinic visit last Tuesday, we

1. Consulted with speech augmentation folks – tried three different units. Kim did great with each.
2. Breathing tested. Kim was 79%. At 50% or lower, need supplemental oxygen.

Kim is getting much harder to transfer.

We agreed on needing to get daily caregiving help. Hoped that Nadine Pennell could do it, but her job just go super busy. We'll get support from a combination of Sharon, Nadine Pennell, and Amy Gillie, while we recruit/search for a full-time answer.

The GoFundMe campaign has raised $28K, with 154 donors. Wow! This removes any pressure on the cost of nursing care, etc.

I picked out a Sleep Number bed, which will be delivered and set up on Wednesday.

The Tobii Dynavox speech equipment trial was delivered today. On Wednesday we'll receive the LC Edge – Eyegaze device to try. Bummed that we were told there is a 3-month wait for the delivery of a new unit.

5:30 – Kim's neck hurts badly.

She peed when Sharon tried to transfer her.

Seems super sad and weak.... like she's dying.

Who am I? How do I want to show up?

Fearless

Clear

Healthy

Giving

Loving

Interested

Writer

Coach

Teacher

Speaker

Encourager

Inspirer

Humble

Born---------------Live--------------------Die

Chop wood

It's just a thing

Why not me?

SPIRIT

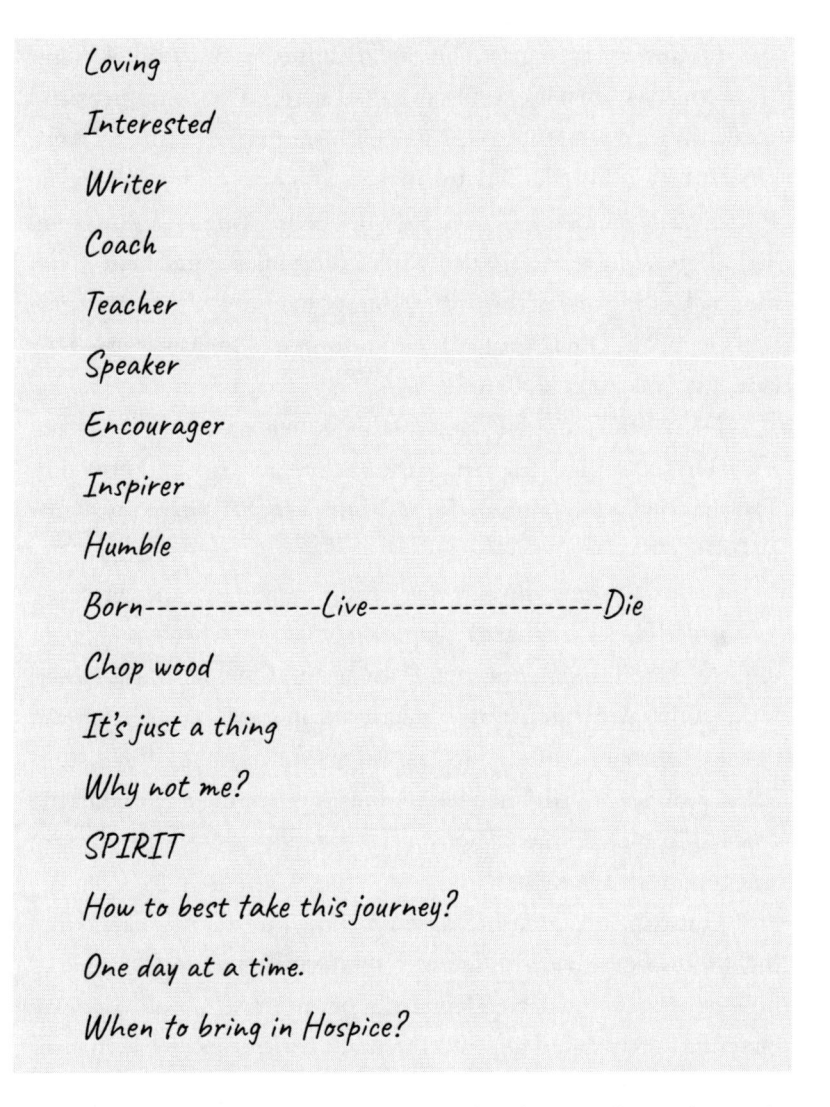

How to best take this journey?

One day at a time.

When to bring in Hospice?

Thanksgiving with Kim's sister's family was planned at Bo's sister's house in Winston-Salem. I was so happy that we had the wheelchair van for this trip. On the Tuesday before Thanksgiving, I ventured to our parking garage to start the van and ensure everything was in good shape for the journey. When I turned the key to start the van, nothing happened. Nothing. Not even a click of the starter trying to engage. Crap!

I found my tiny apartment-style toolbox in our storage closet and removed the battery. I then asked a friend to come over and stay with Kim while I drove to a nearby auto parts store to buy a new battery. I told the clerk the make and model of the van, and he sold me a new battery. I drove back to our apartment building and installed the new battery using my iPhone flashlight held in my mouth. Getting one of the battery clamps to fit over the battery pole was tough, but I finally got it done. I returned to the van, turned the key, and....nothing. Not a sound.

Fuck! I can't take any more of this. Kim is upstairs, dying from ALS. I'm scrambling to prepare the van for our trip, and now this. The shadows were gunning for me, but I blocked them out— for now.

I called the guy who sold me the van and got his voice message. Jude called back later that evening, and I told him what was happening. He shared that he was out of town, and their shop was closed for the holiday. He did, however, have another used wheelchair van in their lot that he offered to loan to me for our trip to Winston-Salem. Awesome! All I needed to do was get our van towed to the dealership, pick up the loaner van, let the folks at Stalls fix our van, and get on with life.

Our trip to Winston-Salem was fine, but the meal and time together were heavy with sadness. I fed Kim, as she was unable to hold utensils. I transferred Kim from her power chair onto a potty chair and then rolled her into the main bathroom to use the toilet. Kim was embarrassed, but everyone put on a happy face. Our drive home from Winston was mainly silent. We both knew that this would be our last road trip.

The following Monday morning, my phone rang. I could see it was the guy from the dealership.

"Hi, Jude," I said as I answered the phone. "How are you today?"

"I'm great. We had a wonderful holiday. How was your trip to Winston? Did the loaner van work okay for you?"

"It worked great. Thanks so much for making that work out."

"No problem. By the way, your van is ready," Jude stated strangely.

"Ready already? What was wrong with it?" I blurted.

"You're not much of a mechanic, are you?" Jude shared without emotion.

Curious and a little angry, I blurted, "No! I'm a life coach. I'm a psychologist. Why?"

"The battery was fine. But you bought the wrong battery. Everything is working great now. You didn't take the plastic cap off the negative battery post before attaching the cable."

In a burst of sleep-deprived frustration, I shouted, "My wife is dying. It was dark in the garage. I'm exhausted. No! I'm not a mechanic!"

He was silent. I realized what I was doing. I apologized.

"No apology necessary. Understood. You can come pick up your van anytime. Just drop off the keys. There will be no charge. We can use the battery you bought on another vehicle," Jude calmly shared as we said goodbye.

Wow. I was such a mess. I couldn't do such a simple repair. I realized how little I had left in my tank for problem-solving and handling issues. Or maybe I was spending all of my problem-solving energy on keeping just a little ahead of the ALS monster, and I was doing well at that. Regardless, it was time for me to go back to Kim.

Saturday, 11/28/2020. ALS Day #214. Clenbuterol day #101. From Journal.

I get stressed by all the details, problems, and grief.

Kim is still asleep.

Our new Sleep Number bed was delivered last week. Kim

seems to like it. It is getting harder and harder transferring Kim:

- o   Powerchair to potty chair
- o   Powerchair to toilet/back
- o   Powerchair to bed/back

Harder to get dressed and undressed.

Kim is losing her speech.

Sunday, 11/29/2020. 7 months from ALS diagnosis. ALS Day #215. Clenbuterol day # 102. From Journal.

Stress is building!

Kim is so sad and angry—and is being so difficult—barking orders at me.

Being a bitch. It is so **HARD**.

I can't stand being ordered around and treated like an employee. I know she doesn't mean to act like this, and I can't begin to understand what it must feel like to be trapped in her body.

My challenge is to better control my thinking and emotions—to where I'm not as affected/reactive to Kim's moods.

Gave full range of motion therapy to Kim – both legs and arms.

Today @ 2 p.m. Magda will visit as caregiver pre-screen/evaluation.

Kim is trying to practice using the Eyegaze system.

BORN·LOVE·DIE

Monday, 11/30/2020 Dana's 35th Birthday. ALS Day #216. Clenbuterol Day #103. From Journal.

Last night was terrible. Kim could not get comfortable and moved to sleep in the power chair at 2 a.m.

At 8 this morning she pottied & moved back into bed.

We used the draw sheet for the first time. Worked well in moving Kim to the middle of the bed and up toward the top. (I'm proud of myself for having the draw sheet and introducing it.)

It is 10:26 and Kim is still asleep.

Today Amy Gillie will arrive at 1 p.m. Kim may want to take a shower before she arrives — but time is running out.

I have 2 coaching meetings today.

Tomorrow — Magda will come for the 1st time. 8:00 – 1:00. Hope it goes well.

I am being forged. In a crucible.

Born--------------------------Live----------------------Die

Chop wood

It's just a thing

Why not me?

SPIRIT

Be present

Be mindful

Be conscious

Be the observer

Wednesday, 12/2/2020. ALS Day #218. Clenbuterol Day #105. From Journal

Today – Kim's dentist appointment at 11:30

Jim Tignor from Tobii Dynavox will come over at 4:00 to pick up Tobii loaner.

Kim is going to choose the Tobii device over the Eyegaze—easier to use. We will order a new one, but I'd like to get a loaner in right away. Kim needs it.

Today @ 5 p.m. we will meet with Tony Johnson – ALS nurse/caregiver. I am very hopeful that Tony will be the right caregiver.

Yesterday from 9-1, Magda came to be with Kim. She was just OK. A little rough with range of motion, plus language issues. I don't like how she looks only at me when talking – treating Kim as if she'd not here. I think most (all?) of her experience has been with the elderly and memory care issues. No experience with ALS.

I'm happy to have our van back—with a new battery.

Need a good caregiver—every day.

I'm starting to lose it.

Did get the Dean's formal approval on my dissertation yesterday.

My Future?

<u>Priorities</u>

o   Caregiver

- o Speech gadget
  1. Order
  2. Loaner
- o Close on the new house
- o Move
- o Decorate

The trip (probably her last one) to the dentist went great. The dental hygienist commented on how clean Kim's teeth were. They were very gentle.

After interviewing several candidates and contacting in-home care services, we hired Tony Johnson as Kim's nurse. Since his retirement, Tony has been a retired Duke nurse, running his own small in-home nursing company. His specialty was with patients with ALS. An answer to our prayers, for sure.

Sunday, December 13, 2020. ALS Day #229. Clenbuterol Day #116. From Journal.

9:00 a.m. Kim is asleep.

I'm reading "When Caregiving Calls." Pretty simple. Not very helpful.

Kim seems to be entering a new level of despair. Super hard to talk. Legs/hips getting weaker. Transfers are getting harder. Left hand weaker – harder to feed herself.

Good things....

Meal train

GoFundMe

Friends / Family

Newhope Church

Tony Johnson – new nurse. Started last Monday. Working Monday-Friday, 8:30 – 4:30 @ $22/hour.

Born ----------------------Live--------------------Die

It's just a thing

Chop wood

Why not me?

I'm OK with it

SPIRIT

Wednesday, 12/16/2020. 4:11 pm. From Journal

I just finished a flight of beers from Southern Pines @ the Oak House. Thanks to Tyler Vet for picking the beers.

Nurse Tony is with Kim until 4:30.

We have dinner from Nana Steak at 6:00, thanks to Virginia Parker.

Today – I had a massage (Wo) from 9:30 – 11:00. Then, a counseling session w/ Rob Womack at noon.

Lunch @ Chick-Fil-A. Checked out progress on the new home.

Grocery – home – helped Kim/Tony with bathroom trip.

Born --------------------Live--------------------------Die

Chop Wood
It's Just a Thing
Why Not Me?
I'm OK with that
SPIRIT

Thursday, December 17, 2020. ALS Day #233. Clenbuterol Day #120. From Journal

Nurse Tony Day #10.

Kim slept until 9 a.m. Said she didn't have a very good night's sleep. My snoring woke her some. Sleep IQ score – 55.

It is getting harder to transfer Kim. I hope we can continue to transfer her w/o using the Hoyer until after we move.

Closing date – 12/31/2020 (14 days)
Move date – 1/4/2021 (18 days)
Patrick arrives on 12/22 (5 days)
Christmas – 12/25 (8 days)
9th Anniversary – 12/30 (13 days)
Receive Tobii device 12/21 (4 days)
Set up Tobii device. 12/22 (5 days)

Live each of these days….one day at a time…. with joy and supernatural peace.

Born-----------------Live--------------------Die

It is what it is

Chop Wood

It's just a thing

Why not me?

I'm OK with this / that

SPIRIT

My goal today --------→ walk in spirit all day long.

I'm going to write a book

I've noticed that I'm more forgetful & absent-minded. I think the relentless stress of this journey is causing that.

Sunday, December 20, 2020. From Journal.

Cold, rainy, sad day.

It is 8:33 am. Quiet. Kim is not up yet.

I'm very sad.

I feel lonely.

It is fucking hard!

Born------------------Live-------------------Die

Chop Wood

It's Just a Thing

Why Not Me?

I'm OK With This.

SPIRIT.

Ashley Thomas came over—in her wheelchair.

> *Kim told Ashley that she wasn't afraid to die, and she wasn't afraid of the progression.*
>
> *She started to say something about how she hated what it was doing to me—and then she fell apart.... sobbing/wailing.*
>
> *Then, I cried. Then, she cried more and turned to uncontrollable laughter.*
>
> *In the midst of all this, I found comfort in hearing her say to Ashley that she was not afraid to die and not afraid of the progression.*

Found on my iPhone notepad, dated December 21, 2020.

She is Gone (by David Harkins)
You can shed tears that she is gone
and you can smile because she has lived.
You can close your eyes and pray that she will come back
or you can open your eyes and see all that she has left.
Your heart can be empty because you can't see her
or you can be full of the love that you shared.
You can turn your back on tomorrow and live yesterday
or you can be happy for tomorrow because of yesterday.
You can remember her and only that she is gone
or you can cherish her memory and let it live on.

Christmas and the day after Christmas (Emily's birthday) celebrations were held at Sharon and Bo's house in Cary. My son, Patrick, was with us, which was awesome. We used our wheelchair van and portable wheelchair ramp, and both days passed without problems. The persistent sadness in the eyes of Kim's mom and dad was heavy. Kim did her best to smile and laugh and lighten the mood.

On December 28, I tweaked my back getting Kim out of bed. I was angry as this was a day that Tony had scheduled not to be with us. We also had a walkthrough lined up for our new house before closing on December 31. The closing was sad. Kim sat in the van while I signed all of the documents for both of us in the attorney's office. A bittersweet "beginning" to our new house?

Thursday, December 31, 2020. ALS Day #247. Clenbuterol Day #134. From Journal.

Last day of this crazy year

Cold, rainy, quiet, sad morning.

I'm reading a book of poetry on bereavement.

8:31 - Kim is asleep

Tony is not coming over today.

11:00 Walkthrough of our new house

1:00 Closing

Big day! Hope it goes well.

A long time for Kim to be away from a bathroom. We'll be fine.

I did buy adult diapers. Kim doesn't know that I have them.

I feel poetry building up inside me.

Born-------------Live------------------Die

It's just a thing

One day at a time

Why not me?

Chop wood

I'm OK with this

What would Dr. Bedlack do?

SPIRIT

My future alone/blank sheet of paper

Exciting	vs	Sad
Healthy	vs	Not
Strong	vs	Weak
Happy	vs	Sad
Powerful	vs	Weak
Love	vs	Fear / Hate
Help Others	vs	Be Selfish

(The left column items are circled together.)

    Our New Year's Eve was uneventful. We watched some shows on TV, followed the normal evening routine, and went to bed early. I reflected on the sad and difficult year we had just finished and sat in awareness that we'd face more of the same challenge in the coming year. I was excited about moving to our new house and looking forward to being able to give Kim a shower in our new, big, wheelchair-accessible master shower.

    We moved into our new house on Monday, January 4. Nurse Tony helped a lot as the movers maneuvered around Kim and me throughout the day. Moving furniture out of a skyrise apartment was tricky, with each load made via the freight elevator another test of patience and endurance. Moving that same stuff into our new one-story home was a snap. After tipping the movers and saying goodbye to Tony, Kim and I settled in to enjoy our first night in our new house.

    We were so blessed that a group of Kim's friends had already delivered, organized, and tucked away all the glasses, dishes, pots, pans, silverware, and all the other stuff for our big, new kitchen. Other friends had assembled the new kitchen table, chairs, and living room furniture that Kim had ordered online months before. Our brand-new house looked so nice.

I heated frozen lasagna courtesy of one of the previous Meal Train deliveries, and we had a glass of red wine with our meal. After dinner, we were both looking forward to the first shower in our big main bathroom. I helped Kim undress, move to the shower chair, and then rolled her in. Everything was so pretty, so new, and smelled so clean. Turning on the water and giggling as I turned Kim around without constriction in the large shower room, I noticed a problem. The water was not getting hot—pure cold water. I quickly went to one of the nearby sinks, and yes, there was hot water. I ran to the kitchen, tried the faucet, and, yes, hot water. Back to the shower, where Kim was naked and waiting in the shower chair—all cold water. I couldn't believe it.

"Crap. There is no hot water," I whispered as I held my hand under the brand-new shower head.

Kim's smiles and giggles turned quickly to screams of agony. Pure screaming hell. This was the worst I've seen of Kim losing control.

"I'm so sorry, honey," I yelled over her ongoing screams. Turning off the water, I went to look at Kim. She was sobbing and gasping to catch her breath. I reached to hold her, and she relaxed in my embrace.

"Do you want to skip the shower or take a quick cold one?" I inquired.

"We have a clinic visit tomorrow. Cold shower…. please. Make it quick," she muttered.

Kim's next (and last) ALS Clinic visit, and time with the famous Dr. Bedlack, was on Tuesday, January 5. Her last hair appointment (and last time to use the wheelchair van) was Wednesday, January 6.

Wednesday, January 6, 2021. ALS Day #253. Clenbuterol Day #140. From Journal

Sitting in my new upstairs office in the new house at The Courtyards.

Kim's breathing test at the ALS Clinic was 69%

Talked a lot about a feeding tube. Kim is resisting. Said she doesn't want to drag this out.

Dr. Bedlack recommended Trilogy (non-invasive ventilator) – which Kim agreed to.

Also, cough assist and suction device.

Start a new round of in-home care. PT / OT.

Start using thickeners for her liquids to prevent choking.

Next appointment – 3/9. 11:30

The following weekend we were blessed with a "home-decorating" visit by Kim's dear friends, Roger and Kelly from Jacksonville, Wulf and Jessica from Austin, Bruce and Jen from Atlanta, and Laura from nearby Cary. This group spent two full days shopping for art and accessories and then fully decorating every room of our beautiful new home. They turned the office into a place for Kim's recumbent bike, desk, and a lit-up string of photos of many of Kim's favorite memories. When they all left the following Monday, the house looked awesome, but the goodbyes were incredibly sad, as everyone knew that time with Kim was short.

A home visit by Ashley, a Pulmonary Therapist with the Duke ALS Clinic, was scheduled. Ashley was sweet, and we all bonded immediately. Ashley explained how to use a trilogy BiPAP ventilator and also explained how to use a cough assist machine. Kim was asked to use the Trilogy during the day, at least four hours per day. Once Kim got used to the ventilator, she could use it throughout the night.

On Friday, January 15, my daughter Dana, her husband Lee, and granddaughter Emmy arrived from Colorado Springs. The three got comfortable in the guest suite upstairs. We all looked forward to a "fun" weekend in our new house. In the weeks before, Kim was having more trouble swallowing some of her meds, especially the large Gabapentin tablets. Dr. Bedlack's nurse suggested that we try a liquid form of Gabapentin.

After saying goodnight to the kids, I moved Kim into our big, beautifully decorated new main bedroom. We could see the full moon shining through the transom window over the French doors leading to the back patio. I transferred Kim from the power chair onto the potty chair and wheeled her into our bathroom and over the toilet. After peeing, I cleaned her and moved her back to the bedroom. After wrapping her in her favorite throw, I gave Kim her normal collection of nighttime meds. For the Gabapentin, we had already talked about using the oral version. Using a plastic syringe, I slowly pushed the liquid Gabapentin onto Kim's tongue. She immediately coughed, and the coughing intensified. As Kim gasped for breath, I could tell she had aspirated some of the medication. Rubbing her back, she continued to cough uncontrollably, fighting for air. I quickly ran to Kim's office and grabbed the cough assist machine that the Pulmonary Therapist had left with us. After trying to use the cough assist twice, with no luck, I went to the kitchen to find my phone and to call the nurse's emergency line. At this same time, Kim quit coughing. Returning to the bedroom, I could see that Kim was breathing deeply and calming down.

"I want to sleep—in the power chair," Kim slurred as she leaned back. "Please move me to where I can see the moon."

"OK. Let me get you dressed first," I whispered, wondering if the kids upstairs had heard Kim's coughing and gasping. I was sure they had, but no one came downstairs to check on us.

By this time in the ALS journey, Kim and I knew how to work together to get her undressed and dressed while in the power chair. Kim could arch her back so I could pull her pants off, and vice-versa when putting on clothes. I dressed Kim in comfortable pajamas and put fuzzy socks on her cold feet. Using the controls on the right arm of the power chair, I tilted Kim back to where she was lying nearly flat, covered her with a blanket, and moved her to where the full moon shone through the window and into her beautiful face.

"Good night, sweetheart. I love you," I said.

"I love you, too," she whispered.

I switched on the white noise machine, with our favorite, the sound of crickets enveloping the room. Turning off the bedroom light, I went into the kitchen and living area to clean up. Later checking on Kim, I saw that she was asleep. I think the kids upstairs were probably asleep as well. Whew, that was a close call. I knew that ALS would gradually affect the muscles in the throat to where it was easy to aspirate liquids into your lungs when trying to eat or drink. This was the first time I'd seen Kim have trouble swallowing. I dreaded thinking about what lay ahead.

I crawled into my side of our empty Sleep Number bed and closed my eyes. What happened with Kim and Gabapentin shook me, and I had trouble settling down.

Beep. Beep. Beep.

"What's that sound?" I thought. Going into the kitchen, I saw that the clock on the microwave was blinking. Resetting it, I noticed that the clock on the front of the oven was also blinking. I turned on the light over the kitchen sink, and it started flickering. Switch by switch, I turned on each of the lights in the kitchen. Only a few came on. Looking out the back door, I turned on the lights over the porch. They worked. I went into the main bedroom, saw that Kim was still asleep, quietly opened the door to the back patio, and tried that light switch. It did not work.

Strange. Some lights worked. Some didn't. Some flickered. Crap! In a brand-new house. *What do I do?* *I'll sleep on it, and deal with it tomorrow.* I crawled into bed and fell asleep.

Two hours later, I woke to the same *Beep-Beep-Beep* sound. As I got out of bed, I noticed it. It was cold. And now there was no power anywhere in the house. I used my iPhone flashlight and looked at the thermostat: 58 degrees. I looked at the weather app on my phone. The outside temperature was 30 degrees. I went back into the bedroom to check on Kim. She was asleep. I felt a cold breeze. Looking to my right, I couldn't believe it. The door to the backyard from our main bedroom was wide open.

My wife has ALS. She is paralyzed. She is asleep in a wheelchair in our bedroom. And her stupid husband leaves the door wide open. Shaking my head at my ignorance, I quietly shut the door, put another blanket over Kim, got dressed, and began to problem-solve the issue. I called the local power company and told them what was going on. They asked me to go to the breaker box in the garage, trip each of the circuits, and report what I saw. The conclusion was that there must be a problem outside the house, and I was told to expect a repair crew by seven the following morning. It was now 3 a.m. Kim was asleep. The house was getting colder. The shadows took up more space in my head, and I could see them mock me as I sat by the gas fireplace. Watching the flames flicker around the fake logs, I pondered my life and what was beginning to feel like me losing all control and confidence in my ability to handle this shitstorm.

The repair crew came the next morning, found the problem in the buried power line by our front yard sidewalk, repaired it, and all was good. Dana, Lee, and Kim all laughed as I shared what had happened the night before. I didn't feel so much like laughing. I was flatly exhausted.

Ever the problem solver, I contemplated how to deal with the Gabapentin issue. Applesauce! Kim loved eating applesauce, using it to help swallow some of her other meds. How about adding liquid Gabapentin to the applesauce before giving it to her? Kim was open to the experiment. Since I loved Kim so much, I thought I'd try it first to ensure it tasted okay. I put 1,200 mg into the small applesauce container, tasted it, and finished it. Not bad. I thought Kim would be okay with it later that evening.

Around 1 p.m., Kim shared that she wanted a nap. I wasn't surprised, given the crazy night we had before. I moved her onto her side of the Sleep Number bed, got her covered up and comfortable, and then undressed and climbed into my side. Reading to her, she fell asleep immediately. I felt my eyes get heavy, and I fell asleep as well.

At 4:30 p.m., I woke with a start. *Where am I?* It was broad daylight, and the bedroom was still new to me. Looking over, I saw Kim wide awake, looking at me with that big, beautiful smile.

"You were snoring," she whispered.

I got up, got Kim up and dressed, and went into the living room. Dana, Lee, and Emmy were at the kitchen table, playing a game. Looking at the instructions on the bottle of liquid Gabapentin, I realized that I had self-administered an overdose of this medication that helped Kim sleep so well. Again—Mr. Stupid shows up. "Well, no harm done, and I got some great rest," I silently counseled myself.

It was wonderful having Dana, Lee, and especially Emmy for a visit. Emmy was such a doll at three years old, and having her around was great for Kim. When it came time for them to leave and head to the airport, a blanket of sadness fell upon the room. First, Kim started crying. Then Dana joined in, with the rest of us completing the symphony of grief. Everyone except Emmy, knew. They knew this was the last time this group would be together. As I do, I watched the clock. When it was already a little late, I shared that we needed to be going to the airport. Tearful hugs and goodbyes were shared; I moved Kim into the bedroom for a nap and quickly helped Lee load up my car with their luggage. Driving to the airport, the car was silent with sadness. Fifteen minutes into the trip, I realized I was going in the wrong direction. After a quick exit and turnaround on the interstate, I headed correctly to Raleigh-Durham International—another brain fart. I felt like I was losing my mind. Luckily, the kids caught their flight, and I returned to the house and my beautiful, peacefully sleeping wife.

Thursday, January 21, 2021. 6:50 a.m. From Journal.

I've Showered

Prayed

Read Bible (app)

Meditated

I've just emailed Stacy Asnani to set up a video meeting with Dr. Bedlack to discuss Hospice with me and Kim. Yesterday morning as I was getting Kim out of bed, I mentioned Hospice, and she agreed.

She is demonstrating behaviors that indicate she is not interested in extending her life:

Not wanting a feeding tube

Not using the Trilogy often

Not trying to use the EyeGaze

My goals have shifted. Now they are:

1. *Be with Kim and do all I can to help her be comfortable.*
2. *Do what I can to see that Kim dies at home*

> 3. Stay physically & mentally healthy
> I think hospice will help with all of this.
> Born---------------Live--------------------Die
> Chop wood
> It's just a thing
> Why not me?
> I'm OK with this.
> What would Dr. Bedlack do?
> SPIRIT

The Zoom call with Dr. Bedlack went better than I expected. Shifting from living with a disease to dying from a disease is such a surreal experience. Somewhere along the journey of ALS, I noticed, or realized, that the doctor would not suggest hospice. I recognized that the doctor's job is to keep the patient alive, period. Or at least that was how I observed the whole system working. Everyone at the ALS Clinic was so nice, steady, helpful, and there for you. But ALS doesn't care. ALS is in the pursuit of one thing—death. Actually, I thought, ALS has two objectives: disability and then death.

Before the call with Dr. Bedlack, I rehearsed what I wanted to say. I wanted to say that the daily challenges, with all the disabilities and struggles, were getting severe. Trouble eating and swallowing. Aspirating. Kim doesn't want a feeding tube. She doesn't like using the Trilogy. The EyeGaze machine is not working well. Communicating is getting harder and harder. Constipation is more of a challenge. Kim is ready to stop the fight. Kim is a Christian; she knows she is going to heaven and is not afraid to die. We think we're prepared to start with hospice.

Dr. Bedlack appeared on the Zoom screen as nice, patient, and empathetic as always. I explained what I had rehearsed and waited for his response.

"I understand," he said. "Hospice is a wonderful part of the journey, and our hospice team is great."

"You do? You understand?" I said with relief, holding Kim's hand.

"Completely. Let me get the process started. The hospice team at Duke is the best, and they are part of my team here at the ALS Clinic. By the way, if you ever change your mind, you can go off hospice and back into our standard care. It's entirely up to you. Why don't you take some time, think about it, and let us know," he said with calm authority and warmth.

I looked at Kim. She nodded her head slightly, but with an intention I understood.

"We don't need time. Kim doesn't need time. She's ready now," I somehow uttered in response. I was aware I was using words I couldn't imagine ever using. My wife was ready to die.

After the call, the air in the room felt different. Like we had hiked up a 14,000-foot summit and finally noticed the cloudless blue sky. The equipment and the anxiety and the daily struggles to maintain abilities, fight the fight, and stay the course.... all of this stress was just erased with one Zoom call, with one decision, with one change of status...on hospice. It felt better. It felt peaceful. It felt like we could relax and move into the next stage.

The first hospice nurse visit was Monday, January 25, 2021.

Saturday, January 30, 2021. ALS Day #279. Clenbuterol Day #164. Hospice Day #6. From Journal.

9:22 a.m. Kim is asleep.

She got some new booties to sleep in, but she kicked them off in her sleep.

We started with hospice last Monday.

Her hospice nurse is Jennifer O'Keefe.

I just texted Jennifer to see if we can get some meds to stop the leg spasms at night.

I paused all of my coaching work. Anna Rosati encouraged me to do this. Feels good. Allows me to focus all of my time on Kim (and me), without feeling pressure to coach people. I'm OK with not making money right now.

I feel like I'm growing spiritually.

Trying to silently, slowly, walk in spirit.

In spirit, nothing can hold me back.

In spirit, I am infinite, powerful, and capable.

In spirit, I have no fear.

In spirit, all I feel is <u>love</u> and <u>strength</u>.

Born--------------------Live--------------------Die

SPIRIT

Kim needs a shower – but we'll see how she is when she wakes up.

I realize that every day will bring new challenges.

- Harder to transfer
- Speaking
- Swallowing
- Coughing
- Dressing

- Toileting
- Breathing
- Pain
- Anxiety
- Depression

My job – be stoic and loving and courageous and there for Kim.

The new house? Nice, pretty, functional

But – just sticks and concrete.

I could live in a tent.

My wife is dying.

Tuesday, February 2, 2021. ALS Day #281. Clenbuterol Day #167. Hospice Day #9. From Journal

I'm cranky and discouraged. I think it is because Kim is hardly able to talk, and I am increasingly having trouble understanding her.

Friday, February 12, 2021. ALS Day #291. Finished Clenbuterol trial. Hospice Day #19. From Journal.

Kim's mom and dad are driving here from Aiken – to arrive at 3:00 pm. Sharon will also come then. They'll stay over the weekend. It will be sad, but necessary.

At 4:00 p.m. we have an appointment/consult with Budget Blinds. The idea is to let Elsie help pick out the blinds.

The hospice nurse (Jennifer O'Keefe) comes every Wednesday @ 3 p.m. She asks:

1. How's your pain?
2. How's your sleep?
3. How's your poop?

Kim has been on Seroquel for sleep the past 2 nights. It seems to be helping.

She is more tired/listless/grumpy during the day.

It is getting super hard to understand what Kim is saying. She is showing **no** interest in using the Eye Gaze gadget.

She is having more choking events, and it is getting harder for her to drink from a straw.

I can hear her breathing is different at night. Sounds more labored.

I don't know how much more time she has, but it feels like the time is coming soon. I'm still guessing March 14, the day after my birthday.

I feel God's presence.

I know that I'm a spiritual being having a very short physical experience.

Born----------------Live----------------Die

How will I live?

Be here now.

Chop wood

It's just a thing

Why not me?

Why not Kim?

I'm OK with this.

What would Dr. Bedlack do?

SPIRIT

February 14, 2021. From Pastor Benji's Facebook Post

Would you please pray for this beautiful couple, Kim and Brett Blair?

As I leave their home today, I find myself having to pull over just to wipe the tears of #joy and #sadness! 10 months ago, Kim was running marathons and crushing the real estate world!

Today hospice is helping us care for this beautiful woman of #God. If you know the Blairs, pls pay close attention, because for those who will have eyes to see, they are showing us how to truly #live and #die...

#ALS

#Psalm23

#HeavenBound

#Hope

BORN·LOVE·DIE

Monday, February 15, 2021. ALS Day #294. Hospice Day #22. From Journal

2:10 p.m. Kim is asleep in her power chair. Has been for ~ 3 hours. Tony sitting beside her on the couch. Watching HGTV.

This morning Elsie & Larry left, and then Sharon left. They were with us since Friday afternoon. Super sad weekend.

Poley's brought dinner Saturday night.

Dan & Amber Lussier / Beth McClendon brought Angus Barn dinner on Sunday night.

Watched the NewHope service on TV on Sunday morning. Pastor Benji came by for a visit on Sunday afternoon. It was a great visit. So good for Kim's folks & Sharon to get to know Benji.

He read the 23rd Psalm and prayed for/over Kim.

My prayer — is that Kim & I both feel God's presence — every moment.

I also pray that Kim can be comfortable during the days that she has left and that she ultimately will die in her sleep.

Idea — have Sharon write Kim's obituary.

I need to start working on what I want to say at her celebration of life.

What Kim has taught me:
- To love all people.
- To put relationships above everything else.
- What I remember most about Kim:

- *Her BIG smile*
- *Her love for people*
- *Her energy*
- *Her laugh*
- *Her strength & courage*
- *Her integrity*

You didn't choose me. I chose you. I appointed you to go and produce fruit that will last, so that the Father will give you whatever you ask for, using my name. John 15:16B

For to me, to live is Christ and to die is gain. Philippians 1:21

In this, you greatly rejoice, though now for a little while you may have had to suffer grief in all kinds of trials. These have come so that your faith, of greater worth than gold, which perishes even though refined by fire, may be proved genuine and may result in praise, glory, and honor when Jesus Christ is revealed. 1 Peter 1:7B

February 22, 2021. From Brett's Facebook Post

As we continue our walk through intense emotions of both gratitude and grief, we are so thankful that Kim can still eat. The awesome meals that you have been delivering have sustained us through this challenging time. I've just updated the Meal Train with dates over the next few weeks.

Please know that Kim, although she cannot speak, is fully

aware of the immense amount of love that is coming her way from all over the world, and she feels your prayers.

Please continue to pray that Kim will be comfortable today, and that one day, she falls asleep, and during an awesome dream, she wakes up in heaven. That will be something to rejoice.

I also feel your prayers, and am personally sustained through this unimaginable journey by your prayers, support, and ongoing friendship.

In grief and gratitude, I am here, knowing you are thinking of us both.

God Bless You All!

Brett

Wednesday, February 24, 2021. ALS Day #303. Hospice Day #31. From Journal

Wow.... the past two weeks have been amazing.

On Wednesday, Feb 17, Pastor Benji made the Ash Wednesday Worship Night message about Kim and Born-Live-Die.

Ash Wednesday.

Come face to face with our mortality. By the sweat of your brow, you will eat your food until you return to the ground, since from it you were taken; for dust you are and to dust you will return. Genesis 3:19

Alpha --- Omega. I am the Alpha and the Omega, the first and the last, the beginning and the end. Revelation 22:13.

Teach us to number our days, that we may gain a heart of wisdom. Psalm 90:12

To live is Christ, but to die is gain.

On Thursday, Feb 18, Pastor Reece Whitehead called me to see if it would be OK if he used Kim's story during his service on Sunday. Yes, and he did.

God's activity is in disruptions in our lives. God is preparing us for something new.

More is less and less is more.

Kim slept until noon on Sunday, 2/21. I thought she might have died, with mixed emotions.

I watched Pastor Reece preach while Kim slept. I cried. Pastor used the analogy of how ancient arrows are made.

Later, on Sunday, Pastor Reece visited our house – for about an hour. It was great. I shared, for the first time in front of Kim, how I've been talking to Pastor Benji about Kim's memorial service, and how it is going to be a big party.

My spiritual growth is profound.

I'm seeing the physical world through my spiritual/non-material/not-of-this-world eyes.

It changes everything.

I feel as if Kim is pushing me to the keyhole, and when she takes her last breath, which could be today, she will pull me through it. At least I hope so.

I want to keep this clarity, this knowing, after she transitions.

Kim is close to being promoted to heaven.

More is less, less is more.

To live is Christ, to die is gain.

Jesus did not worry and hurry.

March 2, 2021. From Brett's Facebook Post

The Bible says...By the sweat of your brow you will eat your food until you return to the ground, since from it you were taken; for dust you are and to dust you will return. GENESIS 3:19.

In other words, Born - Live - Die

We don't have a choice on how we experience birth and death, but we have, if we choose to use it wisely, a huge impact on how we live.

Kim is still with us, and she and I are both trying our best to find joy and peace in the beauty of each day. Kim hopes that you do the same thing, living TODAY fully, with excitement and happiness and gratitude for this thing called life.

May God bless you today, my friends.

Saturday, March 6, 2021. ALS Day #313. Hospice Day #41. From Journal

Using my new fountain pen for the first time

I pray today that I stay in spirit as much as possible this

day. It struck me that all I have control over, and what I most importantly could pray for, is how I experience this day. I know I have influence over that.

I choose to believe in the power of prayer for others, i.e., Kim

I pray that I experience supernatural peace.

I *KNOW* that I can receive that prayer, and experience supernatural peace.

I pray that Kim experiences supernatural peace.

I don't know that my prayer will influence that to happen. Maybe it will. I pray it without knowing.

Faith? Hope? Belief? ---→ Maybe

Born--------------------Live----------------Die

The human experience

Kim is still breathing.

I live time now with the awareness that I need to be prepared for her to breathe or not breathe.

I'm OK with this.

Why not me?

More is Less. Less is More.

More "stuff" of this world pulls me away from knowing and living who I really am. I am a perfectly created spiritual being having a very short physical experience.

"Let everything happen to you: beauty and terror. Just keep going. No feeling is final."

~ Rainer Maria Rilke

Human life is short. It is an ongoing unfolding of experiences. These experiences are received through our senses, our brains, our thoughts, emotions, and feelings. Our senses are very limited in their capabilities.

- Sight
- Hearing
- Taste
- Smell
- Feel
- Intuition

Sunday, March 7, 2021. ALS Day #314. Hospice Day #42. From Journal

I am a spirit being experiencing physical doing.

I'm walking in a bubble of time and space

I am the one who is observing the experience.

I woke up at 2:30 – couldn't go back to sleep. Got out of bed at 4:30. Took a nap on the couch upstairs.

The visit yesterday with the crew went OK (Elsie, Larry, Sharon, Bo, Emily, Tommy, Marsha, and Jeff). Then, visit with Siobhan Hunter. Sio brought lasagna. Kim choked on the lasagna. Super scary. Kim is exhausted.

I pray that today I am continuously aware that I am a spiritual being having a physical experience. I will experience **today**, with Kim, with love, patience, presence, calm, paced, courageous, confident. Today is just a piece of fiction, a bubble in time and space – that will come and go. It is not real. I am simply an actor in this drama. Play my part well.

Monday, March 8, 2021. ALS Day #315. Hospice Day #43. From Journal.

Nothing too bad happened over the weekend.

She did eat the same lasagna for lunch on Sunday. We watched the church service together on Sunday. Then, she took a long nap.

Visit with Dan/Amber/Clara Lussier – they brought dinner.

Kim's last bowel movement was 3/2 (6 days).

I'm looking forward to Patrick and Jen's visit on Saturday. (3/13 – My 60th)

Also, Mom and Mark arrive on 3/14 and stay through 3/16.

March 11, 2021. From Brett's Facebook Post

Hello Friends,

Kim and I continue to be amazed at your generosity (and awesome skills in your kitchen) as we've benefitted greatly from the meals over the past few months.

Kim can still eat (such a blessing) but does best with foods that are soft and easy to chew. She really can't eat bread, vegetables, soups, or anything spicy. (Now....for me, I can eat anything, and I do! Thank you very much.)

I've just updated meal dates for the rest of March. Kim and I look forward to being blessed by your food, and if she's up for it, a short visit when you drop by.

Please know that Kim is napping more and more these days, and has other nursing and care needs that may interrupt her ability to see you when you deliver your meal. She hates not being able to visit with everyone, but we know you understand the circumstances.

We continue to find joy in the simple moments of each day, and are doing this thing called "life" one day (really, one moment) at a time. I'd recommend that approach to anyone. It is simply the best way to live - not regretting or holding on to the past, and not worrying about the future.

In grief and gratitude, we are blessed to call you, our friends. God Bless You All!

Brett

Friday, March 12, 2021. ALS Day #319. Hospice day #47. From Journal

Woke at 4:45. My stomach was making noises.

Up at 4:55 - tried to leave the room silently.

My bare feet click on the floor, and sometimes my bones click.

Tony is not coming today. Sharon is coming at 8:30. I'm looking forward to seeing her.

March 13, 2021. My 60th birthday. From Journal.

I woke up at 5 and went upstairs to read. I heard Kim on the baby monitor around 7 a.m. She muttered "Brettita." I ran into the room, and she was wide awake, with a smile. As I got closer, she struggled to say "Ha....y bir...day." "Haa...bee bur daaay". With a tear, I said "Thank you!!!!" I love you so much!!

Yes, it's my 60th birthday. You are so sweet to wake up and wish me a happy birthday. Do you know what time it is?

She shook her head – no. I said, it is 7. You are up so early. Would you like to go back to sleep? She nodded (yes), I kissed her on the lips and left the room.

It was eerily silent. I couldn't hear a thing from the baby monitor. 8, 9, 10, 11.... still no sound at all. I thought, did she wait until my birthday, say happy birthday, and then die? I convinced myself that this is what had happened. I thought I'd wait until noon and then go into the bedroom to check on her. At just before noon, I heard on the baby monitor, "Brettita." I went in, she was wide awake, and said she needed to go to the bathroom.

BORN·LOVE·DIE

Friday, March 19, 2021. ALS Day #326. Hospice Day #54. From Journal:

    Kim slept until 11:00.

    I had coffee with Reed at 7 a.m. He brought flowers and a cupcake.

    Tony here.

    Sharon here.

    Kim laughing out loud watching Derry Girls.

    We will have the memorial service at NewHope Church on a Saturday.

    Kim will be cremated at Hall-Wynne Funeral Home in Durham.

    Urn will be Hudson Blue ($325)

    Cremation service is $4,265

    Keeping urn @ St. Michael's Catholic Church $3,600

    The birthday weekend was hard. Mom was amazingly selfish and negative/whiny. Mark was great. Patrick and Jen were great! I like Jen a lot! They got me a nice bottle of bourbon and a big German Chocolate cake. Patrick and Jessica Harrell put "Happy Birthday" letters in the backyard. Mary Justice brought over a cake from Nantucket Café. Amy Baldwin brought balloons. Reagan Pruitt gave me a bottle of Maker's Mark.

My super-power? Staying in knowing that I am a spirit being having an experience as a physical doing/thinking/feeling.

How to explain this? I don't know. God? Yes ------→

At my spirit dimension, which is here NOW and always has been and always will be – I am perfectly in alignment with God. Powerful. Infinite. Only one description. Love------→

I LOVE God.

I LOVE other people.

I pray that I walk with God – in every step that I take. With this spirit connection, there is nothing on this physical plane that can affect me – not at my spirit level.

Not Kim's disability

Not Kim's suffering

Not Kim's death

Not my death.

I'm OK with all of this.

Why not me?

Born--------------------Live----------------------Die

Not in my control. What do I do with this? Not in my control

Live more and more in awareness of and in alignment with my spiritual dimension.

Experience every day on this earth-bound physical

dimension fully, with joy, happiness, love for myself and others, with courage and confidence.

Live each day without worry or hurry.

From March 21, 2021, From Brett's Facebook Post:

I'm getting bombarded by people lovingly asking what they can do for me and for Kim. Here is my answer:

Just pray.

Pray that I feel God's supernatural peace with every step I take today.

Pray that Kim feels the same with every breath she takes today.

Pray that one day Kim dies peacefully in her sleep.

We feel your love. God Bless You.

Tuesday, March 23, 2021. ALS Day #330. Hospice Day #58. From Journal:

Watching concrete being poured on a new house behind ours.

Listening to Wayne Dyer.

Kim makes gasping noises now and then.

Texted Anna Rosati – hoping we can talk.

Hospice nurse Jennifer approved Kim using morphine every 3 hours – for pain.

Kim does not want to use it.

I misunderstood Kim – thought she had back pain when getting out of bed – she said it was bed sores. She wanted 2 Advil. I thought it was for pain. She said it was to be ready for range of motion exercises.

Sam Poley made me an appointment for my first COVID shot, which I got at a small church in Rolesville.

Kim asked me to invite Amy Baldwin over for dinner last night. Kim coughed a lot.

Kim wanted a full Klonopin last night.

My job – stay present and experience all that shows up today without worry or hurry.

Confident and calm.

Accepting and aware.

She is coughing while in bed – seems to be struggling/uncomfortable.

I don't know when to give her morphine.

<u>Funeral Plans</u>

If possible, on a Saturday

Celebration of Life

Pastor Benji – religious service

Tim Thorpe to suggest Bible verses and music

I like "To live is Christ. To dies is Gain."

"More is less. Less is more."

Born----------------------Live----------------------Die

Speakers: Brett Blair
Tim Thorpe
Sharon Degnan
Kelly Morton / Jessica Sullivan
No statement about ALS
No pictures of Kim with ALS
A PARTY
Kim was not afraid of death, because she knew where she was going. This knowing, this faith, allowed her to live more fully.
What would Kim want?
For people to smile more.
For people to get along better — to love each other.
To prompt people back to church
To prompt people to try out church
To get people to live each day fully, and not take one day for granted.

From iPhone note – March 23, 2021
Kim Pain:
Lower back while sleeping
Neck & shoulders when transferring
Head and neck when adjusting the power chair
Arms and shoulders when dressing

Pain in legs when raising them to get undressed.

Thursday, March 25, 2021. ALS Day #332. Hospice Day #60. From Journal.

I am super sad today.

I think caregiver fatigue is setting in.

Yesterday was sadder and more difficult than before. Maybe because Hospice folks came, and we talked about using morphine. Kim doesn't want to use it yet. Communicating is harder than ever. Kim doesn't want to visit with people.

I must wake up every day prepared to:

Care for Kim – physically and emotionally, or

Plan her funeral, etc.

My challenge—be OK with either path. To fully accept what shows up. To experience what shows up without worry or hurry. To experience what shows up with love. Love with God. Love with other people.

I am a spirit-being, also doing a short physical …. experiencing a short physical doing on this little spinning piece of rock called Earth. I am the observer of this experience. My challenge – experience today well.

I feel better now.

Sunday, March 28, 2021. ALS Day #335. Hospice Day #63. From Journal.

Facts:

- Kim can barely talk
- She can barely drink
- She is sleeping more and more
- Sunday night the very first time in 335 days that she has gone to bed early.
- It is getting very hard to pull up her pants
- Questions:
- Did we have our last shower?
- Can I continue to be Kim's 24/7 caregiver until she dies?
- How much longer will this go?
- Will my back hold up?
- Will my emotions hold up?
- Do I need to hire additional help?
- When/or will Kim take morphine?
- When will Kim stop eating or drinking?

7:45 p.m.

Just put Kim to bed, after reading her two chapters of Ordinary Grace.

Kim is so incredibly sad, exhausted, and cannot speak.

Today she woke up at 11:00 but didn't eat anything until 2:00.

We took a shower. She can barely stay in the shower chair, and it was very hard getting her dressed.

She woke at 8:30 a.m. and wanted the Sleep Number bed made softer (35)

Looking back – Friday was terrible.

Tony put too much thickener in Kim's water and in her coffee. She got super frustrated and started screaming. Twice. We sat out on the front porch, and I fed her lunch there. Long, hard, sad evening.

Saturday morning, I talked to Nicole Bell who encouraged me to move Kim to a hospice facility. I also talked to Sharon and Anna Rosati about it.

Kim woke up at 2 p.m. Sharon came over for a visit.

I went to the grocery and Moe's. We had an OK day.

Tuesday, March 30, 2021. ALS Day #337. Hospice Day #65. From Journal.

Kim woke up at 10:30. Pretty happy.

Chose to wear pajamas – top & bottom.

Eat – ½ bowl oatmeal. Very little juice. No coffee.

Asked me about her Medicare application. I told her that it was approved, but that we will keep our insurance through Hunter Rowe / UHC and put Medicare as secondary. That Hospice is 100% covered under Medicare. That I reviewed this with Brent Stubbe—he advised I keep things as they are. Extends my COBRA period and preserves the life insurance opportunity. Kim got angry and told me that she wanted to know these things.

Kim wanted to buy a lamp for my side of the bed. We did it online through Wayfair.

She wanted to make sure I apply for the 2nd $750 grant with the ALS Association.

She wanted to know if we were OK financially, and I explained that we were.

She wanted me to find the Psalm 23 book, and for Sharon to read it to her – maybe on Friday.

I showed her the text photo of rings that Maddie and Catie made from Kim's first wedding ring.

I flossed and then brushed her teeth. Her gums bled a little.

When moving from the toilet chair to the power chair, she said I could start using the Hoyer lift if I wanted.

She wanted to move the Trilogy ventilator out of the living room – out of her sight.

From iPhone Note – March 30, 2021.

ALS

Born – Live – Die

Chop Wood

It's Just a Thing

Why Not Me?

I'm OK with this.

What would Dr. Bedlack do?

SPIRIT

How to make meaning of this?

It is what it is.

Let go and let God.

Be a source of joy and pleasantness each day.

Love one day at a time.

Don't think about the future.

Don't think about the past.

Connect to our spiritual essence and love that part of our connection.

Pray for a miracle of healing.

Pray that I feel God's loving presence.

Pray that Kim feels God's loving presence.

Pray for Kim's peace, safety, and happiness.

Make the shift from "doing" to "being."

Chose love over fear.

Start with God.

Stay with God.

End with God.

Everything is impermanent.

Everything passes.

Nothing remains.

Nothing lasts.

Only the whole endures eternally.

Saturday, April 3, 2021. ALS Day #341. Hospice Day #69. From Journal.

Sharon, Elsie, and Larry visited yesterday. Went pretty well. Elsie can't help herself but talk non-stop about trivial things. I think it is her way of coping with the grief. I can't imagine the pain that she's feeling. They are all coming back over sometime today.

I had a super spiritual experience while in the shower this morning. I realized that my life on earth is a dream—it is not real. What is real is my eternal spiritual essence. And I realized that my "dream-state" physical body here on planet Earth can also experience other dreams while sleeping. Last night I dreamed that Kim was pregnant, with ALS. And I haven't had sex with her for over 4-5 months—I can't exactly remember the last time it happened. Strange dream.

Today is seven days since her last bowel movement. Yesterday Kim could drink and eat (blessing).

She seemed more sad and tired than ever.

Took a nap in her power chair—in the living room—after everyone left - ~ 1 hour.

Super quiet and nice.

I'm shifting my thinking to now expecting Kim to live until the end of April.

One year with ALS. 4/29/2021.

That is 26 more days. I can do it.

My goal—experience each Earth day feeling God's love and give out love to other people. Period.

From April 4, 2021, iPhone Note:

Reach out with love

Do your best

Do not be concerned with outcomes

Love dissolves fear

Monday, April 5, 2021. ALS Day #343. Hospice Day #71. From Journal:

- Joy
- Ease
- Lightness

Beautiful sunny day—high of 75

Had a pretty good weekend. Kim's folks, along with Marsha, Jeff, and Sharon visited three times.

Kim did pretty well. Smiled and laughed a lot.

Kim can still eat, still drink, barely talk, and not notice/complain about breathing.

Sleeping and napping more.

No morphine yet.

How much longer? I woke up at 1:30 thinking she had died.

Her stomach was making strange noises, and I couldn't hear her breath at all.

I finally heard her breathe, and I later fell back to sleep.

I need to stop trying to guess/predict when Kim is doing to die. Just be here now, doing one day at a time. Do today without worry or hurry.

Be calm and confident.

Love God. Feel God's love. Love Kim. Love others.

Thursday, April 8, 2021. ALS Day #346. Hospice Day #74. From Journal.

I had a bad night's sleep — woke up almost every hour. At 6:00 Kim made a big/loud sighing/gasping noise, and I could hear fluid in her throat. Then, she went back to sleep. Yesterday with Jennifer — The hospice nurse. Her pulse ox was 98. Blood pressure good. Lungs clear. Jen heard coughing and told me that was her aspirating.

Getting Lidocaine Cream for pain across her neck/shoulders.

I don't like how Anna Rosati has distanced herself. It is probably for the best. I shouldn't depend on her or any other humans. I should depend only upon myself and God.

I know I can finish this race. I can land this plane smoothly.

Here. At home. In our house. Kim is getting so weak—sleeping more—hard to talk. Coughing more. No real pain. No morphine yet.

How many more days? It doesn't matter—I'll be here, and I can endure as many days as she has left.

I just told her "I love you."

Sunday, April 18, 2021. ALS Day #356. Hospice Day #84. From Journal.

Yesterday Kim tried to drink twice and couldn't.

She didn't want any food.

She did take her meds with apple sauce.

She slept until 11:00.

Napped in our room from 3:00 – 5:15.

Back in bed at 9:30. Kim was more sad/distressed/angry/exhausted than ever.

This morning I talked with Kelly Morton and filled her in. I think Kim will die sometime this week.

Pastor Benji sent me a text – asking to come to visit – YES!

Sharon will come over tomorrow. I'll get my 2nd COVID shot tomorrow.

Born----------------Live------------------Die

The die part can be messy.

My job today:

Care for Kim

Grow spiritually

BORN·LOVE·DIE

Pastor Benji visited on April 19. (The last photo I have of Kim)

Wednesday, April 21, 2021. ALS Day #358. Hospice Day #87. From Journal.

Mostly no food or drink now for 9 days.

I had coffee on the porch with Brent Droege

Tony coming today at 10:00

Sharon coming today at 12:30

Jennifer – The hospice nurse coming at 3:00

Kim is declining. Other than applesauce, and yesterday a few bites of banana pudding – no food. Very little water. So sad watching her try to drink.

How much longer can this go? I pray that she dies today. Yesterday we watched TV together all day.

When I'm not caring for Kim, care for myself by growing spiritually.

Born----------------------Live----------------------Die

Friday, April 23, 2021. ALS Day #360. From Journal.

Kim is breathing.

Gasping more often.

I pray today that I walk in full power and know of my unblocked full spiritual connection to God.

Today I will:

1. Care for Kim

2. Care for me
3. Pursue spiritual growth
4. Love other people

Yesterday Kim was in bed until 2:30. I read to her for part of the afternoon.

Drank a few sips. No food other than applesauce with meds.

Watched TV. The Voice and five movies.

My challenge: Be blissful, whole, and confident—no matter what shows up today. Bring laughter and joy to Kim's experience.

I can do this.

No longer trying to predict when or how it is going to happen. Let that go.

Let go and let God take over.

April 24, 2021. The first dose of morphine.

Sunday, April 25, 2021. ALS Day #362. Hospice Day #91. From Journal.

A beautiful, sunny Sunday morning.

Had coffee with Sam Poley.

Had a terrible night's sleep. Kim was gasping much of the night.

Yesterday Kim asked, for the first time, for morphine. It made her relaxed, but she did not fall asleep.

We watched five movies.

Sharon came over for part of the afternoon. Kim had a little Gatorade, and no food, other than applesauce with her meds. She did enjoy a watermelon ice pop.

I hope that today she'll take more morphine. Maybe she'll stay in bed all day / most of the day. Maybe she'll go to heaven today. I pray that she does. She has suffered long enough.

I laid in bed with her at 9:00 and read to her.

Tuesday, April 27, 2021. ALS Day #364. Hospice Day #94. From Journal.

Yesterday Kim took two doses of morphine.

I slept pretty well last night.

Sharon came over for a visit.

We watched six movies.

I had coffee with Reed this morning. He's such a good friend.

I'm listening to Kim breathing on the monitor. Today is day #15 with no food.

I'm wondering if today is the day. I hope so.

The full moon shone directly on Kim's face last night.

I told her how much I loved being her husband.

She cried.

I read from A Gentleman in Moscow, then turned on the crickets, light out, sleep.

Thursday, April 29, 2021. One-year Anniversary with ALS. ALS Day #366. Hospice Day #95. From Journal:

Had a terrible night's sleep.

During the hospice nurse visit yesterday, in front of Sharon and Tony, Kim shared that she wanted to stop eating applesauce because she wanted to die.

She was very worried about constipation. Jennifer told her that morphine would make her constipated. Kim went to bed with no morphine, or any of her other meds, except oral Klonopin.

I overslept on my coffee date with Reed. When I went to the porch at 7:15, he was sitting there, waiting on me. I told him everything that had happened. He said, Kim will die today. That made me feel good.

I had Tony stay upstairs. I asked Sharon not to come over (Kim's idea).

Yesterday I got so frustrated that I asked Sharon and Tony to leave the room when Jen was dealing with Kim, meds, morphine, etc.

Kim is ready. So am I.

Saturday, May 1, 2021. ALS Day #368. Hospice Day #97. From Journal.

I'm sitting at the kitchen table, enjoying the sunlight on my face. Listening to Kim breathe on the baby monitor. Her breathing is changing a lot. Some gasping. Some light snoring. Some whistling? Long periods with no breath at all.

If she wakes up, and if she wants it (which I will encourage), I'll give her morphine.

I know Kim is near the end. She is ready. So am I. The waiting is nerve-wracking.

Yesterday, when I moved her to the poddy chair and then to bed, I noticed that her legs are more stiff and rigid than ever. I pray that God takes her home to heaven today. She has fought the good fight. It is time.

9:15 she called for me. Asked for morphine. I gave it to her, got in bed next to her, then fell asleep for 1.5-hour nap. She is now breathing softly but irregularly.

Monday, May 3, 2021. ALS Day #370. Hospice Day #99. From Journal.

Kim is still hanging on.

Hospice visit yesterday. Now on morphine every two hours. Haloperidol every six hours. Hyoscyamine every four hours as needed for secretions.

Kim is running a fever. I think she has pneumonia.

Sharon was here most of the day yesterday.

I thought Kim had died last night. I heard a ticking noise coming from her lungs after each breath.

She woke up around 2:30 a.m.—moaning. I got her into her

power chair—gave her meds—moved to the living room, and we watched four movies.

I told Kim that it is OK to go ahead to heaven.

Sharon will tell her the same this afternoon.

End of Journal entries.......

On Tuesday morning, May 4, I called Hospice nurse Jennifer and told her Kim was having more trouble with pain and breathing. She said she would consult with the Hospice team and get back to me. She then came by the house at 9 a.m. She seemed different when she walked into our foyer. She walked faster than normal, and I could tell she had something on her mind. Kim was in our bedroom, asleep. Jennifer gently woke her, asked how she felt, and checked her pulse and blood pressure. Kim fell back to sleep.

In the living room, Jennifer shared that the doctor at the hospice center wanted to speak with me over the phone. I agreed; Jennifer dialed the number, shared a few words, and handed me her cell phone.

"Hello, Mr. Blair," said a pleasant voice on the other end, "How are you doing?"

"I'm exhausted, but I'm okay," I replied.

"I'm sure you are. I know this is tough. Mr. Blair, we believe it is time," the doctor followed. "We feel Kim will pass soon, and we'd like to increase her morphine and other meds, so she'll be fully sedated and not experience pain."

I felt a wave of sadness and relief. Kim had been fighting the fight for so long and had lived much longer without food than anyone had predicted. I was ready for her to be done with the suffering. But I was not prepared to say goodbye.

"Jennifer will come by daily or more often if you'd like. She'll give you new instructions today on the meds to administer, and we'll have them delivered to your home," the doctor said as I barely attended to her words.

Kim will pass soon. Those unthinkable four words kept replaying and bouncing between my practical, ready-for-this-struggle-to-be-over brain and my exhausted, broken heart.

"How much longer does she have?" I quivered into the phone as I felt a tear on my left cheek.

"We don't know—it could be anytime now. Hours or maybe a couple of days," the doctor replied with a combination of stoicism and care. "If others want to see her, you should tell them today."

"Okay, thanks. I appreciate your call," I numbly muttered as I tried to come back to alert caregiver mode.

I called Sharon, and we both cried. She came over early that afternoon. I called Patrick, who had recently moved to Charlotte with his new girlfriend, Jen. Two weeks earlier, Jen had accepted a travel nurse position in Charlotte so they could be near Kim and me when this dreaded time came. It was now time. Patrick and Jen drove to Durham with her two dogs and arrived at our new house early that evening.

Kim's medications were more than tripled in dosage, and morphine was given every four hours, around the clock. Jen, an experienced emergency room nurse, was a godsend. Already exhausted, the challenge of providing meds every four hours to my dying wife was a new level of despair. Jen and Patrick took over the evening shift. Welcome to the family, sweet girl. Patrick did good!

On May 6, Nurse Tony, whom I delegated to the background for most of the past few weeks, took charge. Having been through this story with several patients before, he insisted that I get some rest and that he would take over 24/7. Tony's wife brought his clothes and toiletries. I moved into the first-floor guest room. Kim stayed in her power chair in the owners' suite. Patrick and Jen and the dogs moved upstairs. Tony slept on the couch at night between med times.

May 7, 2021. From Brett's Facebook Post

An update on how our sweet Miss Kim is doing:

This lady is a fighter! Kim remains with us, at home, and is still breathing (very shallow breaths) and her (STRONG) heart continues to pump. She is heavily sedated with a combination of morphine, Haldol, and Ativan, and is hopefully feeling little or no pain from what her body is experiencing in these final hours or days.

Kim is receiving 24/7 nursing care from Tony, our awesome in-home nurse whom we've benefited from since December, with meds being administered orally on an hourly basis. She is also being closely monitored by the folks with Duke Hospice.

Kim's trip to heaven could occur at any time, and when that happens, she will be free of the suffering of this last year with ALS.

While we will all miss Kim terribly, we should also all rejoice in the end of her suffering on earth, and be happy that she is residing in her amazing new home in heaven.

I know that Kim would like as many people as possible to attend the celebration of her life. This service will be held on Saturday, May 15th, at 2 p.m., at NewHope Church in Durham. If Kim continues to hang around here on Earth a little longer, we may need to reschedule the service for the following weekend.

I am so proud of Kim. She has fought the fight with grace, dignity, courage, and love. She never once felt sorry for herself, and always put other people first, up until the very end.

> *For me, I will be OK. I look forward to seeing everyone at Kim's celebration of life service. I thank everyone for your ongoing love and support.*
>
> *Kim loves you. I love you.*
>
> *God Bless you, our friends.*

Kim didn't die in hours or a couple of days.

Seven days later, on Tuesday, May 11, the Duke Hospice Team suggested we move Kim to the Hock House Hospice facility. This was to administer drugs better "intradermally" and change the medications as needed to help Kim go ahead and pass. Nurse Jennifer shared how she and the others on the hospice team had never seen someone go so long without food or water. It was clear that Kim's heart and lungs were unusually strong. I knew she wasn't afraid to die, but my God, how she unconsciously hung on to life. I was proud of her and amazed by her fighting spirit.

The paramedics arrived at our house. Jennifer suggested I not watch the transfer from the power chair to the stretcher. Patrick and I made bourbon drinks and exited to the backyard. Fifteen minutes later, Nurse Tony returned and said that they needed help. I went into the kitchen, bent over, and lifted my sweet, now so small Kim from her powerchair onto the stretcher. It was my final act of service to my amazing wife.

I offered the recumbent bike to Tony, and he enthusiastically accepted. Patrick and I helped move it into the bed of his pickup.

The next few hours were a blur. I was so thankful that Patrick was with me. He held me up.

Patrick and I went to the Hock House facility and visited Kim. We met the amazing staff there. They asked if Kim would like her hair washed. I said, "Yes!" Kim soon started being more relaxed, and her eyes began to close. She looked much more at peace. I leaned over her face, kissed her on the lips, rubbed back her clean hair, whispered, "I love you, babe," and said, "See you later." Holding back tears, I left the room.

Sharon and Bo then came to visit Kim. Patrick and I went to the Pour House for beers and met with Reed and Sam at Mother's & Son's for dinner at 6:30 p.m. At 8:20, I got a call from the hospice facility, and the nurse told me that Kim had passed. I cried out loud on the sidewalk in downtown Durham and was held up and hugged by my two friends and my son.

Reed, Sam, Patrick, and I finished dinner and returned to our house for more drinks.

I slept alone in our bed for the first time in over a year.

Kim's celebration of life was four days later, on May 15, 2021. Over 500 people attended in person, and who knows how many people watched online. It was an amazing event celebrating the life of an amazing woman.

Chapter 6

♡

IRONY AND THE ACADEMIC

I DON'T REMEMBER WHY, BUT FOR SOME REASON, BACK IN 2011, I bought the book, *Flourish* by Dr. Martin Seligman. Reading this book changed the trajectory of my life. My life coach, Dr. Tom Hill, suggested I make a habit of reading and keeping track of the books I read. I've done both. Ever the engineer, I created a spreadsheet and tracked the books I bought and the books I read. I still do this. Same spreadsheet for sixteen years. A great habit that I highly recommend.

As a young adult, I spent some time interested in self-help stuff. I read Dale Carnegie, Napoleon Hill, Earl Nightingale, and Wayne Dyer. I watched the movie *The Secret* and checked out *The Book of Miracles* and Marianne Williamson. I remember being interested in the possibility of aliens, flying saucers, lost civilizations, and ESP and near-death experiences. While working in the buttoned-up, so-called security of the corporate world, where rules are set, and the paycheck is regular, part of me was curious and exploring other aspects of life and culture. I remember rejecting the notion of "get-rich-quick" schemes and sticking to the pathway of steady, hard work. I was annoyed by the pyramid schemes some friends and neighbors pitched. I began to view "self-help" books and their creators as phony, fraudulent mechanisms used to take advantage of weak people who couldn't make it in the real world. I did, however, know that I had a unique sense of positivity and optimism and had some sense that these traits were working to my advantage. I was curious. I was seeking something deeper.

The book *Flourish* shifted my perspective on positivity, optimism, and "self-help." In reading this book, I learned about a new science called positive psychology and a new theory of well-being called PERMA. I realized that many of the ways in which I was already living my life were now scientifically proven to be part of the PERMA framework for living a good life. According to this book, if a person grows in the five aspects of PERMA, they are more likely to live a life of well-being and happiness: a life that flourishes, and a resilient life. That was the life that I wanted. I soaked up every word of this book and wanted more.

The five letters in the acronym PERMA are short for:

P – Positive Emotions

E – Engagement

R – Positive Relations

M – Meaning

A – Achievement or accomplishment

I then went on to read more about positivity and more books written by Dr. Seligman. By this time, I was also learning more about coaching and had gone through a coaching training program offered by my friend, Dr. Roger Hall. As part of this amazing program, I was required to research and write an academic paper on a subject of my choice. I chose *resilience*. I recognized that my life has been full of challenging situations, both personal and professional, where I needed a high degree of resilience to carry on. Everyone will face serious difficulties at some point, and resilience will be necessary. I became an avid student of this topic. I read about the ancient Stoics and other famous examples of living with resiliency.

I was now recognizing the growing impact that Tom Hill had on my life as my coach and how his philosophies were molding me into a better version of myself. Tom had developed a 52-week coaching curriculum, which I had completed twice. I started casually coaching other people, following the same process that Tom Hill used with me, and I began to notice life changes happening in the folks I was working with.

I later signed up for Brendon Burchard's "Certified High-Performance Coach" program and became licensed to coach under his trade name. With a different curriculum aimed specifically at the habits of high performance, I began to integrate these frameworks with the ones taught by Tom Hill. I started coaching people for a fee and set my prices at the same amount I had been paying Tom. I'm so thankful for this because I entered the coaching world charging much more than most beginning coaches. I didn't know any different. It worked—for me and my clients.

My interest in positive psychology continued to grow, and I read, or rather devoured, more books. As I researched more about Dr. Seligman, I learned about a formal program on positive psychology that he chaired at the University of Pennsylvania. I discovered a master's degree called MAPP, Master of Applied Positive Psychology, taught personally by Dr. Seligman. Wow! This grabbed my attention. I recognized how crowded and unregulated the "life coaching" world was. I thought earning a university-level education and credentials would help me be more qualified and credible from a marketing perspective. I started to fill out the application for the MAPP program.

My next coaching call with Tom Hill was coming up. I was excited to share with him my plans for the MAPP degree.

During our call, I told Tom what I had in mind. He was quiet and listened. Then, as all good coaches do, he asked a question.

"Don't you already have a master's degree?" he inquired.

"Yes. I have an MBA from Tennessee State University," I replied.

"Then why don't you get a Ph.D.?"

Coaching. The art of asking powerful questions. He did it again.

I hadn't even considered a Ph.D. But it was a brilliant idea. My eyes shifted as my mind moved into overdrive. That would be awesome. I loved college, I enjoy a challenge, and there's no way to be more credible in the coaching space than to have a "Ph.D." after my name.

"I don't know," I shared. "I hadn't even thought of it. Let me look into it."

"Well, tell me what you find out," Tom replied, then continued to our other coaching topics.

I soon learned that no Ph.D. programs in positive psychology were offered in the U.S. The field was just too new—a few master's programs, like the one at the University of Pennsylvania, but no Ph.D. After a few more days of research, I landed on the Ph.D. in industrial-organizational psychology offered at Capella University. This accredited online program could be finished in five to eight years, and I could do the coursework on my schedule, maintaining my coaching and recruiting businesses simultaneously.

I finished the application. In November 2015, I was accepted into the doctoral program. The next four years were a blur. My brain has never been stretched so far and wide. At times the program seemed like looking into a black hole. Reading more than humanly possible. Learning to navigate the world of academic research. Becoming proficient in quantitative and qualitative analysis and synthesis. Learning about my own biases. Growing as a critical thinker. I could start to observe my growth and was thankful for it.

After three on-site dissertation preparation weekends, I had to identify my dissertation topic formally. My first idea excited me. I wanted to conduct a quantitative study on how coaching can affect resilience. I've been interested in resilience forever, and the engineer in me wanted to do a dissertation where I could show off my skills with statistics. I was confident the coaching work I had done with many of my clients had helped them become more resilient, and I could see how my Ph.D.-level study that confirmed this would differentiate me as a coach.

I proudly and confidently presented my dissertation idea to

the chair of my dissertation committee. Sharing with enthusiasm how this research idea could make such a big impact, my professor listened intently. Then, she popped my balloon. To have "statistical significance," my study would need to involve at least one hundred participants, each of whom had experienced coaching. For ethical reasons, I could not include individuals I had coached personally. To get any real sense of impact, I would need to survey participants before and after a coaching period, ideally one year or more apart. In addition to the costs and effort required to recruit such a large number of participants, I would also need to identify qualified coaches and pay the coaching fees. My advisor tried to soften the blow as I shook my head in deep disappointment at the costs and time required for this great study. She said the good news is that I could get a grant to help with the costs or get a student loan. Also, she reminded me that I had four more years to complete the dissertation.

Fuck. I didn't want to do this thing for four more years. I also didn't want to try to get a grant or borrow money. I had already paid off all of my first student loans. I couldn't imagine how much work it would require to find one hundred people to volunteer to be coached, and who knows how many coaches to work with these people. Frustrated and exhausted, I watched my cool dissertation idea dissolve into history.

"Or," my advisor continued, "you could do a qualitative study. Several students have done interesting qualitative dissertations, and the university is becoming more accepting of these lately."

I hadn't even considered a qualitative study. The engineer in me was defaulting to quantitative research, where I could test a hypothesis and use the results to predict outcomes. A qualitative study seemed too soft and fuzzy, and unscientific.

Over the next few weeks, I re-read previous classwork on qualitative research and read several qualitative dissertations. I became newly aware of the power of this approach to psychological science. I also was reading books by Dr. Brené Brown and became interested in the newest research on the topic of *shame*. I learned that Dr. Brown was a qualitative researcher and also that she was a very highly paid speaker and consultant. I thought about how cool it would be to model my career in her direction.

I proposed a qualitative study on how people experience job loss to the university. One of the rules in dissertation research is that you need to study something that has yet to be researched specifically. Your job as a researcher is to find a "gap in the research." This is so hard. To find a "gap," you need to know all that has been previously researched. This is nearly impossible, but so is getting a Ph.D. Yet after spending hours and hours in the online academic library, I found my gap. I would study how middle-aged corporate male managers who were laid off from their jobs and successfully found jobs later experienced the whole layoff and rehire process. I could conduct a study like this with only ten to fifteen participants, and it would require only a one-hour recorded interview with each. I could do all the work myself and finish in six months, not years.

However, the topic did not excite me. It did not inspire me. I didn't expect to grow from it or do anything meaningful with it. I was previously an HR guy and laid off many people. I owned a recruiting company and helped many men find new jobs after a layoff. I had coached several people through a layoff and finding a new job. I knew this space very well. I could see how doing qualitative research based on good interview questions and skills could help me as a coach. Other than that, I saw this study as one that would be easy, boring, hopefully quick, inexpensive, and simply a means to an end. The final step in completing this marathon called a Ph.D.

My dissertation plan was approved by the Institutional Review Board (IRB) at the university in November 2019. Whew! Finally! I was ready to recruit participants, conduct the interviews, do the analysis and the literature review, and finish this. Kim and I were excited about moving to our skyrise apartment in downtown Durham in mid-December. I would conduct my qualitative interviews in person in my office at the Frontier in the nearby Research Triangle Park.

My study's participants were recruited primarily through placing Facebook and LinkedIn posts. I needed to find at least twelve. The first four volunteers came quickly, and then no more. Oh, no! I changed my posts a bit and also reached out to well-connected friends in the Raleigh area, asking for their help. Two more participants volunteered, but I still needed to get the required number. By the end of January, I was starting to panic. How do I get more participants? My advisor suggested expanding the age range and asking the IRB if I could use video recordings instead of in-person meetings to interview participants. As such, I could recruit participants from across the country. I hoped to recruit some people from my ten years in Detroit. I modified my dissertation research plan, re-submitted it to the IRB portal, and crossed my fingers.

Weeks went by, and I was still waiting for an answer. I knew the university, as old-fashioned as it was, expected that all qualitative research be conducted in person. Formal training was offered on observing body language and facial expressions when asking the carefully designed interview questions. I learned that body language was almost as important as the words themselves. I began to fear that the IRB would flatly deny my request, and I would be stuck.

Friday, March 13, 2020. My fifty-ninth birthday. As I mentioned earlier, Kim and I had a blast that night. On Sunday, March 15, we learned that Durham would be in lockdown on Monday. Lockdown? You have to be kidding me. We were just getting comfortable in our cool apartment in the middle of the city. Kim was still new in her real estate career but was crushingly busy with listings and buyers. We had just bought her a new Toyota Rav4, which she loved.

A week later, an urgent announcement was transmitted by the university. I cautiously opened the email. Because of the uncertainty of the pandemic, all in-person activity, including classes and human research, was to be terminated immediately and replaced with telephone or video conferencing if possible.

Bam! My lemon was turned into lemonade. The IRB soon approved my request to use video interviewing. I modified and expanded my Facebook and LinkedIn recruiting posts and quickly obtained the five additional volunteers for my research. With twelve participants, I could start the research phase of my dissertation.

Still considering my research project uninspiring, I set about conducting the interviews on Zoom. As I read the news, I learned about more and more companies around the country and the world having massive layoffs due to the pandemic. Looking out over the quiet city of Durham from our ninth-story apartment, I began to sense that my study on layoffs may have real practical application in the current and coming economic situation.

I conducted one-hour recorded Zoom interviews with three of the participants in April. The results were interesting. With each interview, I found myself looking forward to the next one. I was anxious. With qualitative research, the researcher must identify repeated themes that emerge during the participant interviews. In layperson's terms, I hoped to hear similar stories from several participants. My hopes came true. My boring, uninspiring research project quickly moved from something I just wanted to get done to something interesting, to applicable, to emotionally moving, to deeply personal.

At 4 p.m. on April 29, Kim was diagnosed with ALS. You've already read the story. Everything changed. But I was looking at the finish line on this Ph.D. program. Kim wanted me to finish it. My future self wanted me to finish it as well. Finish it I would.

The remaining participant interviews were conducted, with more interesting findings. Kim continued to work in her real estate business and carry on as best as she could, with steadily worsening symptoms and increasing paralysis daily. After finishing the twelve interviews, I carefully listened to each recording while meticulously transcribing the words into Word documents. I had not anticipated how much time this would require, but I also noticed how deeply I connected with the shared stories. I was pleased that each participant shared similar stories and experiences. Obvious repeated themes evolved out of the analysis of the interview transcripts and were confirmed by re-watching the recorded Zoom videos. I was thrilled with the results in terms of their value to my last step in the Ph.D. program, but another realization was bubbling up inside of me.

I realized that the themes that emerged from my study could be a road map for my surviving and recovering from the trauma of caregiving for Kim and her upcoming death. I told no one. I just thought about it—deeply.

The five themes that emerged from my research were described in great detail in my final dissertation report. Each of the men who had personally experienced job loss reported:

1) **A Dark Journey.** There was no shortcut to this. Regardless of their education, status, financial position, and confidence, every man went through a period of deep despair, loss of identity, shame, and anxiety.

2) **A Blessing in Disguise.** Every participant reported being thankful that this unplanned trial was forced upon them. They recognized the growth that took place. Several noted they became better leaders, husbands, fathers, and humans. They were thankful for being forced to learn new things, join a new team, learn about a new industry, and develop new skills.

3) **Role of Family.** The men in my study leaned heavily on their young and grown children and their wives or partners to get through the trauma of job loss.

4) **Importance of Professional Network.** Eleven out of the twelve participants found their next job through someone they already knew.

5) **Meaning.** Many of the participants were eventually offered several positions. Everyone ensured that the job

they accepted would allow them to contribute to something bigger than themselves meaningfully. They were more concerned with contribution than their paycheck, title, or career growth.

As I marinated in the complicated analysis phase of my research while at the same time experiencing the rapid changes in Kim's health, I had an awakening. I recognized that my ability to maintain PERMA in my daily life and remember the themes that emerged from my research could be my roadmap for navigating the trauma and grief of the caregiving journey and Kim's death. The twelve participants in my study were, without knowing it, my support group. I made a private commitment not to allow this trauma and tragedy to ruin me, as is the case with "learned helplessness," but instead use it as a curriculum and journey of personal resilience and post-traumatic growth.

I also recognized the irony of this whole situation.

I've forever been interested in resilience. My research project as part of my first coaching program was on resilience. I've read every book I could find on resilience. I've coached people on resilience and tried to grow in my habits to build resilience. When it came time to do a dissertation for my Ph.D., I chose resilience. And soon, I began to hear from other men who were each resilient; my gorgeous wife of ten years, in the absolute prime of her life, gets diagnosed with a shitty terminal disease.

Lights out.

Everything changed.

It's like God said, "Okay, Mr. Positive. You think you're so resilient? You think you got this? Let me test you. Try this."

And I did. I cared for Kim. I loved Kim. I spoke at the celebration of her life. I'll miss her forever.

But I tried to apply the five elements of PERMA in my life during her illness and afterward. They helped.

I tried to follow the five themes that emerged from my

dissertation research during her illness and afterward. I still am. They helped and are still helping.

And I'm thankful for the twelve men in my study, many of whom are still my friends, as they were unknowingly my support team. They helped.

And I still love God. Deeply.

Chapter 7

♡

BORN – LIVE – DIE

DEATH.

Death is such a strange thing.

I had dealt with death before, but not at such an intense and intimate level. And not for such a long time, minute after minute after minute, moment after moment, with all of the ugliness of it right in front of my face. I couldn't have imagined caregiving for someone who knows they are going to die, but here I was, doing just that. Doing what I couldn't have imagined. I don't think it's something you can prepare for. You just do what shows up. I tried my best to do it well and to do it with love.

It was surreal. There are all of the practical things that you do as a husband and caregiver, which I'll write about in the next chapter. Thank God for practical things, as they are an escape from the deep, sad, emotional, unthinkable things. The roller coaster of fear and grief and horror and wonder and awe and curiosity and love and more.

In the privacy of my own privacy, I was subliminally searching. I felt like I was alone at midnight in fog-filled woods, carrying a dying flashlight, searching for a way out. Trying to make sense of all that was happening. Trying to find a way to cope and survive and maybe grow and not fall completely apart.

Thankfully, as the disease progressed, Kim was able to sleep pretty well. Through a combination of prescription meds typical for ALS patients, terpene shots from The Happiest Hour, and at times a hit or two of cannabis, Kim could usually fall asleep and sleep throughout the night. We had developed a nice bedtime routine where I would get her in bed and comfortable on her side, and then I'd get in bed on my side and read to her. I'd then kiss her goodnight, turn out the lights, and play nighttime sounds of crickets or frogs or rain or ocean waves. After a full day of caregiving and carrying the physical demands and emotional stress that grew each day, I, too, would close my eyes and fall fast asleep. I thanked God for sleep. We both did. Kim sometimes dreamt of running in her perfectly healthy body. Sleep was our place of escape. We both wished we could stay there.

But morning would come. My nighttime dreams would soon be replaced by the nightmare of the day ahead. I'd wake up around five a.m. I could never fall back asleep. My mind would start processing all of this all over again. I was proud of how ninja I was becoming. I could wake up, slowly crawl out of bed and out of the bedroom without making a peep. Kim never heard me. It's amazing how quiet we can be if we move slowly and with intention.

Over the ten-plus years before, working with my coach and as a coach, I had developed a solid routine for the morning. I was proud of my routine. It worked well. I get up early, make coffee, write down my goals, pray, read from the Bible, meditate, and write in my journal. These activities, these behaviors—these were foundational for my daily productivity and growth and joy and setting the stage for magic that reliably showed up in my life until now.

Now.

Now I was in a whole new ballgame. Dealing with the unthinkable.

I remember a morning in June during the year of ALS like yesterday. I went out on the balcony of our ninth-floor apartment with a cup of coffee, journal, and iPhone and sat down. It was dark. The city below was quiet, as it was still in partial shutdown mode with the pandemic. I heard a dog bark in the distance. I heard a siren. I listened to the train coming. The sound of the train made me think about the sound as it roared past our house when I was a kid. Even though the train would rattle the windows in our small house, and if it derailed, it would certainly crash into our house, I found comfort as a boy with the rhythmic sound of the train rushing by and the reliability by which it came by every evening and every morning. The train was my childhood friend. Thinking about those memories made me smile.

And then, my happy memories of my awesome childhood dissolved as my mind shifted to more happy memories. Happy memories of the past ten years with Kim. Alone on the balcony, with a slight summer breeze tickling my eyebrows and with my eyes gently shut, I felt the beginnings of a tiny smile develop at the corners of my lips. It felt good to smile. It felt good to feel good. But as quickly as the happy memories appeared in the story in my mind, it all shifted to dark. Memories of Kim running across the finish line at the City of Oaks half marathon were replaced with Dr. Hawes saying, "I'm sorry, but you have ALS." Catching my breath, I began to sob. Outside in the dark, crying like a baby. My mind spun in the pain and sadness of such a wonderful marriage to such a wonderful lady, a true love story—a story that was over or soon to be over.

I knew I had to change what I was thinking about. Get out of the past. I instinctively moved to think about the future. That's worked for me in so many other situations. I'm eternally optimistic. Dr. Hill has taught me that the best is yet to come. I've studied positive psychology. I coach people on dreaming about the future, writing down their dreams, and then turning their dreams into goals to then watch them come true.

So, I began thinking about the future. It didn't help. I cried even harder. Looking into the future was even worse. With my eyes still shut, I watched a mind movie where Kim would be increasingly more disabled. She would lose her ability to walk. She wouldn't be able to talk. She would be stuck in her body, with her mind fully awake, have trouble breathing, suffer, and somehow die. And then, I would be alone. I would miss her. I would be lost in the dark. And with all of this spinning in my mind, I cried. With my chin buried into my heaving chest, I sobbed.

Tilting my tear-stained face upward, I slowly opened my eyes. The eastern edge of the dark sky before me was turning pink. A bird flew overhead. I could hear the faint sounds of cars and trucks on the highway. The top edge of the rising sun was peeking just over the horizon.

I took a deep breath. And then another. I watched the sun as it ever-so-slowly but steadily rose into the morning air. I breathed again. Another bird flew by, joining the first bird in a playful game of sky tag. I felt my frown-filled face move to neutral and then back to a slight smile.

A smile? How in the hell could I smile? I realized how. The present moment. Be in the present moment. I realized that it wasn't so bad when I put my mind on the present moment and took it out of the hell of reliving the good and bad memories of the past or being anxious about the future. It wasn't so bad here in the present moment.

I breathed again. I smiled again. I looked at the continuing rising of the sun and the bustling city below. I listened to the sounds. Like, really listened. I smelled the cool, moist air and felt the chair my butt was on and the cup I held with my right hand. I took a sip and tasted the coffee. I looked up and said thank you. And then silently, I said to myself, "This is it, Brett. This is where it is. This is where I can go, where I can be, to escape the pain of this sad story. Be here, in the present moment."

And then I had a wave of knowing, of inspiration. I recognized that the best way I could serve Kim through her remaining days was to be a joy-filled partner living in the present moment. I could sense the power, clarity, and bliss that could come with that kind of life. I realized that my ability to be in the present moment would not only help me to be the best partner for Kim but would also be the best way for me to be the best version of myself, launching forward after she dies.

Somehow, and I don't know how, Kim did the same thing. Even before she got sick, Kim lived mostly in the present moment. This presence of hers was amplified during the year of ALS. She smiled every day— literally, including the day she died. She chose to make the best of each day—each moment—that she had left. Maybe it was through her example that I found this same remedy.

I decided. I decided to live the rest of my life that same way.

After doing my morning routine, I would shower and get dressed. All of this was before Kim woke up. I would use the little shower in the hallway bathroom so Kim wouldn't hear me.

I've always done some of my best thinking while in the shower. Often a solution to a problem I've been wrestling with will appear while under the water. During the year of ALS, my thinking mind— my mind that was previously so good at solving problems and setting goals, and getting stuff done—this mind was buried somewhere below the part of my mind that was searching for sense and meaning.

The shower was a place of respite. A short vacation. An escape from the non-stop burden. A place to let my mind wander and my body rest.

I stared at the shower tiles in front of me. Dozens of them. Maybe hundreds, who knows? I didn't bother to count. The part of my brain searching for meaning saw an analogy. Each of the tiles could represent a person. Each person was a tile, and the grout line above each tile represented the timespan for that person's life. With my right pointer finger, I reached out and touched the grout line on the top left side of a tile up and in front of me. I slowly traced that grout line, gently sensing the roughness of the grout, and said to myself, "Born, live, die."

"Born, live, die," I repeated as I traced the top grout line on other tiles.

It hit me.

Everyone on planet Earth has the same story. The story is one of being born, living a while, and then dying.

I thought of people I knew who had died. My grandma Besse died. I vaguely remember her funeral. My younger sister Tracy died of breast cancer way too early, leaving three small kids. That sucked. My father-in-law, Ralph, died. That was a pivotal moment in my life. My ex-wife, Carol, died. That was so, so sad. I knew several others who had died, some from old age, some from disease, some from accidents. It became so clear to me that everyone dies. Everyone. Everyone who has ever stepped foot on this planet. Everyone here now. And everyone yet to be born. They all die.

And this includes Kim. And this includes me.

I touched a tile in front of me. I said to myself, "This is Kim." As I slowly traced the top of the tile, from left to right, I said, "Kim was born, she's alive, she's going to die, but she hasn't died yet."

A deep breath. Looking for courage. As I continued to trace the tile to the right, I said, "When Kim dies, which will be sometime soon, she will be free of this pain, and she'll be in heaven." And then I thought, "But she is here now, and so am I."

I turned to the right, facing the wall running lengthwise to the tub. With my right hand, I placed my palm in the center of one tile. As I patted that tile, I said, "This is me. I'm here, now." Tracing the top of the tile, from left to right, I said, "I was born, I'm living, I will die, but I'm not died (misspelled intentionally) yet. I'm here, now, today, and I have a choice. I choose to live fully, knowing that I am both a spiritual being and a physical being. My spiritual side is unaffected by the ALS journey, and my physical side will die one day. But probably not today. Today, I have a choice."

With the hot water pouring down my back, I would remove my hand from the wall, look up to the ceiling, and say, "Thank you.

Thank you, God. Thank you for creating me with both a spirit and a body. Thank you that I know the difference. Thank you that I know who I am. Today I pray that I can feel your love, knowing that my assignment is to feel your love and release it to other people."

I would then turn the water to cold, count to one hundred, turn off the water, dry off, get out of the shower, brush my teeth, get dressed, and get on with the day.

My "Born-Live-Die" process evolved as Kim's disease progressed, which you've read in my journal entries in Chapter Five. I'll share more in the next chapter – about caregiving.

I discovered my morning routine to be a lifesaver as a caregiver during the year of ALS. I also found it a powerful way to reset my presence and faith and gain clarity of who I am and what I'm here on Earth to do and be. I still follow this morning routine, minus the part about saying Kim will soon die. She did die. I am sad.

Chapter 8

♡

CAREGIVING

IF YOU LIVE LONG ENOUGH, I'M GUESSING YOU'LL EVENTUALLY find yourself in a caregiving role. Caring for an aging parent is a common scenario many people enter. With the weird combination of modern science allowing for people to live longer but an epidemic of chronic disease making people live less healthily, the caregiving challenge for seniors is maybe at an all-time high. For people who are born helpers, caring for another human being may be a natural talent or inclination, something they enjoy, and even a career choice. Nurses, hospice workers, physical and occupational therapists, home care aids...these folks are angels, and I'm so thankful for them. I'm not a natural "helper," so learning to be a caregiver took some time.

Other than some short stints of caring for my first wife's medical needs, I never faced serious caregiving until I received a call from my mom in 2010. I previously shared the story. At 66 years old and widowed, my mom was diagnosed with idiopathic pulmonary fibrosis (IPF). IPF is an incurable lung disease, and in my mom's case, it was quickly leading to her death. Her only chance of living more than a few months required her to receive a double lung transplant. Her pulmonologist in Florida recommended that she look into the lung transplant program at Duke University Medical Center in Durham. Long story short, Duke would only accept Mom as a patient for this complicated procedure if she had a full-time caregiver, preferably a family member, live with her in Durham. The caregiver needed to be on call, 24/7, to be able to transport her immediately to the hospital when the donor's lungs were harvested. At 49 years old, bald, broke, and recently divorced, I moved to Durham with my mother and began an unplanned, full-time caregiving journey.

When a caregiving assignment randomly knocks on your door, you need to immediately drop or juggle other activities and priorities in your life. I was running a recruiting company in the suburbs of Detroit. I loaded my computer and clothes in my F-150 pickup and drove to Durham. My mom and I rented a dingy little apartment in the shadows of the Duke medical complex, where I did my recruiting work remotely from my tiny apartment bedroom. I didn't tell any of my clients that I had moved. My mom needed to lose serious weight before the lung surgeon would place her on the transplant waiting list. Every morning, I would drive her to the Duke Center for Living, where she would work with physical therapists. The goal was to get stronger while losing weight, which is uniquely difficult when the patient cannot breathe. Over several weeks, Mom ate like a bird, nearly starving herself. She also stoically pushed a shopping cart around the indoor track of the fitness facility, wearing a mask connected to two oxygen tanks, and monitored by the therapists after each lap. I did the shopping, cooking, cleaning, and laundry and accompanied Mom to her doctor visits, tests, and procedures. I was also her amateur therapist as her stoicism was replaced with tears and fear, exacerbated by her steadily diminishing ability to breathe.

A few months into this caregiving journey in a strange town, I got the nerve to set up an eHarmony online dating account. With no idea how long I'd be living in Durham, it felt like the right time to try to meet someone, maybe. I wasn't searching for a committed relationship, as I knew I'd return to Detroit once my mom's situation changed. "Changed" meant she hopefully got a transplant and could return to Florida. The other option was one I did not want to think about.

I met Kim on eHarmony on July 1, 2010. Mom lost weight and was placed on the official transplant waiting list on July 29. On July 30, matching donor lungs were harvested, and Mom was called to the emergency room for the much-anticipated surgery. Through a procedure that I still do not fully understand and consider a miracle of modern medicine, a pair of healthy lungs from a deceased donor we know nothing about were meticulously placed in Mom's chest cavity, replacing the old lungs that were so diseased. Kim, my brother Mark, and I looked down at Mom as she opened her eyes after eight hours of surgery, breathing independently with her gift of new lungs. Two months later, after completing an exhaustive post-surgery rebab program, Mom was released from Duke. I packed Mom's stuff and drove her back home to Florida, where she could start a new chapter of life without struggling to breathe.

With all organ transplants, the patient trades one problem or disease for other health challenges. The tradeoff is for a lifetime of taking a cocktail of medications that help the body avoid rejecting the donated organs. This is done by confusing and weakening the immune system. The unfortunate side effect is being more susceptible to other problems, like infections, diabetes, kidney failure, and cancer, to name a few. Mom took on this challenge like a champ and was militantly compliant with taking her medications, getting blood tests, pulmonary function tests, bronchoscopies, and a battery of other interventions developed to increase the odds that her new lungs functioned well and long into the future.

I loved my mom fully, but we were very different and got on each other's nerves. A visit for a few days was pleasant. Living together in a tiny apartment with the stress of a fatal disease hovering was terrible. During that time of caregiving for my mom, exercise, work, and spending time with Kim, whom I was falling in love with, were my escape. Returning Mom to her home in Florida, with good health, was awesome. I could breathe deeply again. I could start to live again...in the present moment and into the future. I could dream. I could smile. I thanked God for all this goodness.

Caregiving for my mom was over! Whew!

Well...not completely.

Even though Mom was now back in Florida, the Duke Lung Transplant team wanted to keep close tabs on her and her new lungs. She was asked to come back to Duke regularly, at first every three months, then every six months, then annually, to evaluate her lungs and overall health. Mom fell in love with Duke and demanded that she go to Duke doctors for any health-related issues. Over the next ten years, Mom made twenty-five trips to Durham and stayed with Kim and me in our guest room for each visit. I was her caregiver for each episode. While she thankfully never experienced the rejection of her new lungs, she did suffer a stroke, a heart attack, a near-death atrial fibrillation episode, two hip replacements, surgery on the arteries in her legs, and surgery to reroute arteries to her heart. I could drive to the Duke Hospital with my eyes closed. The doctors and nurses became my friends.

Mom's home in Niceville, Florida, was near my brother, Mark, and his wife, Gretchen. Mark and Gretchen took great care of anything Mom needed during her time at home. I took care of anything Mom required when she was in Durham. While Mark and I never talked about it, we had a well-functioning caregiving partnership, and we respected each other's roles in doing our parts well in caring for Mom.

The caregiving journey for Mom thankfully transitioned from one of 24/7 intense life-or-death support to episodic doctor and hospital visits, intertwined with good times with good health. Life regained some normalcy, and I enjoyed my new life in Durham, married to Kim, and growing my coaching career.

Then came ALS.

Kim and I both already knew about ALS. We both knew that she would die from it. And we both knew that it would take the two of us to navigate it. With the diagnosis came my commitment to taking care of her. My new priority was clear—to be the best caregiver I could be until the day she died.

Mom's health challenges continued. Mark and Gretchen didn't flinch. They immediately took over all the caregiving roles for Mom, including traveling with her when she had doctor visits, tests, and surgeries at Duke. This cleared the way for me to focus 100 percent on Kim. I'm so thankful to Mark and Gretchen for this.

Caregiver. I was now a full-time caregiver…again. But, this time, it was with the woman I love, my wife. And I was caring for a person who knew she would die. We both knew it. That was such a twist in the plot. The knowing. Or maybe not? We were both Christians. We both believed in the miracle of healing. But we also both believed in science and the facts on Earth. Both of our minds shifted to cycling about all the questions and unknowns. Death. Heaven. Sadness. Frustration. Grief. Hurt. Disbelief. Fear. Faith.

I'm not a caregiving expert. I've had some experience, but that's all I have. But I do feel like I did it well, really well—well for Kim and well for me. Therefore, I think I have some expertise to share. And I've seen others do it so poorly—poorly for the person being cared for and poorly for the caregiver. Both made me sad.

A big part of caregiving is physical work, and maybe a bigger part is psychological. I don't know which is more or harder, and perhaps it shifts around or is different in different people with different situations. I knew that my job—my purpose, was to be with Kim, to help Kim, to encourage Kim, to be pleasant and be a beacon of positivity and joy, doing all I could to make her as comfortable as possible while minimizing her suffering during the ALS journey.

I do know this. Being a caregiver for a prolonged period can ruin the caregiver. Don't let this happen to you. Kim didn't want ALS to destroy me, and I didn't want it either. I knew, or hoped, that I would be able to be a great caregiver for Kim and stay healthy enough through it to be there for her needs until the day she died.

I also hoped I could be healthy enough to have a sound body and mind for whatever was in store for me in my life after Kim died.

On the "taking care of Kim" side of the assignment, I was supported immensely by the program of care developed at the Duke ALS Clinic. Led by Dr. Bedlack and supported by his entire staff, Kim was wrapped in a cocoon of loving support. Kim's health and self were monitored from the day of diagnosis until the day she died, and we were both held up and encouraged. A full book could be written on the intricacies of the ALS Clinic support services. From a caregiver's perspective, having many things to do and people involved helped immensely with the psychological horror of living with and watching my dear wife slowly die. "Things to do" included going to physical therapy, occupational therapy, speech therapy, pulmonary therapy, and clinical exams. It included recording Kim's voice, swallowing tests, taking meds and supplements, participating in a clinical trial, fundraising for ALS, designing and building a new house, buying different wheelchairs, buying a wheelchair van, trying out various speech generation devices, using a cough-assist machine, buying an adjustable bed, getting a Hoyer lift and learning how to use it, being trained on range of motion exercises, interviewing and hiring an in-home nurse, trying to use a ventilator, meeting with a lawyer and updating wills and creating a family trust, making funeral plans, and some travel to family and friends.

In some ways, all this physical stuff of dealing with ALS was the easiest part. The harder part, for me, and I think for Kim, was sitting and being with the disease when nothing else was happening.

When Kim was diagnosed, we agreed that we would live each day, one day at a time, and do it with joy. We both knew that she was going to die and that we only had so many days left. We set about doing just that—living life one day at a time.

But I had a private plan. While I agreed that we would live life together one day at a time, I secretly was living one and a half days at a time. By this, I mean that I was always looking ahead to the next thing that would show up in the ever-progressing (or declining) nature of the ALS disease so I'd have the necessary equipment, tools, or answers ready. I wouldn't tell Kim. This became a fun challenge—most of the stuff I bought on Amazon. I purchased furniture risers to put under the couch and chairs to make her getting up easier. I purchased a lift kit for the toilet. I bought a pole to put in front of the toilet that Kim could use to pull herself up. A brace for her wrist, utensils with foam to make them easier to hold, a better pillow, rails for the side of the bed, shoes that were easy to put on, a clock that displayed the time on the ceiling, a baby monitor so she could call for me, a wheelchair ramp, bars for the shower, the next book to read to her, the next puzzle to work on, the next friend to come visit, flowers, the next meal, the next Bible verse, the next prayer.

For me, having a daily routine was a huge part of maintaining sanity and stability during the year of ALS. Most important was my private morning routine. You've already read a lot about my morning routine through my journal entries previously shared.

A daily reset of what's real, what's important, talking to God and getting settled before Kim woke up—that sustained me. It also changed me. It formed me. It helped me be a better caregiver and also helped me to become a better person. Usually, in the shower, I'd mentally revisit all that was going on, and got to a point where I would repeat a set of statements, mantras, that helped. You've already read these in my journal entries. Let me expand:

Why not Kim?

Somewhere I read some wisdom on the question many people ask themselves when bad things happen to their loved ones. "Why did that happen to her?" one might say. I reminded myself that we live in a random universe with bad things happening to all kinds of people—good people and bad people. So, why not Kim?

Why not me?

And the same logic applies to me. Why should I be immune from bad things happening? Plus, I think I'm pretty resilient and capable of handling the tough stuff. That's another reason for "Why not me?" Maybe someone else couldn't take it.

Chop wood.

This was my mantra for showing up every day, and "doing the work." The relentless, hard, stressful, sad work of caregiving for my dying wife. Just do the work as if I were chopping down the trees in a huge forest—one chop at a time, sometimes with a dull old axe.

I'm OK with this.

This reminded me that all is unfolding as it is meant to unfold, according to God's plan. Just relax and let it flow. Don't resist. Be at peace. Breathe.

It's just a thing.

This specifically concerned the upcoming hard things I knew I would need to do for Kim one day. Things that I couldn't imagine doing and things I didn't know how to do. Like putting on her makeup, wiping her bottom, shaving her legs and under her arms and her girl parts. Like using the Hoyer lift. Like administering morphine. Like writing her eulogy. It's just a thing. Be stoic and do the things.

What would Dr. Bedlack do?

This was my reminder that Dr. Bedlack (and his team) were always only a phone call away, and I could get answers to anything that showed up in this crazy journey. I knew that Dr. Bedlack had worked with thousands of patients with ALS, from their earliest symptoms and diagnosis all the way to their deaths. This comforted me.

SPIRIT

This was where I always landed during my morning self-talk in the shower. This was my code word for remembering that I am both a physical body and a spiritual being. And Kim was the same. And for both of us, our physical bodies will die, but our spiritual beings will continue. There is no ALS, caregiving, sadness, or burden at the spirit level—just pure love. Reminding myself of this made me smile and helped me step into the day with more patience, care, and love for Kim, myself, and others.

In addition to having a daily morning routine that included time for prayer and meditation and taking time for myself for exercise, the most important thing to surviving the caregiving year of ALS was to surround myself with the support of other people. Consistent with the PERMA theory emphasizing the importance of positive relationships, and my dissertation findings discovering the importance of family support and professional relationships, I ensured that I didn't get too isolated with Kim and the ALS challenge.

I leaned heavily on my son, Patrick, and my daughter, Dana, for love and support during the entire year of ALS and the months after her death. I can't imagine how I would have survived without both.

Kim's sister, Sharon, was a constant source of support—for me and Kim. Sharon was nearby or with us from the day of diagnosis until the day Kim passed. She was my rock. I can't thank her enough for her steadfast love of Kim and me, and I will forever cherish our friendship.

I mentioned earlier that Anna Rosati was a lifeline for me. She eventually found out about Kim's diagnosis and immediately reached out to us both with her love and concern. Anna also contacted me privately and offered her support in any way. I soon met with her in the coffee shop on the street level of our apartment building. I hadn't seen Anna for several years and was nervous about how this would go. As Anna approached, she looked at me. I returned the look. With no words said, we communicated through our eyes and silence. We both knew. We both knew ALS, and both knew the journey. She had experienced the full journey, and I was somewhere in between. When we talked, I felt heard and understood. Anna was my living example of resilience and surviving ALS as a caregiver. Over the coming nine months, Anna also spent several afternoons alone with Kim, giving her a much-deserved laughter-filled break from me and giving me a much-needed break from the relentless caregiving burden. Anna and I remain great friends, and I will forever be thankful for the love and support she provided Kim and me.

I've already written about the blanket of support provided by the care team at the Duke ALS Clinic. In addition to the support that each provided directly to Kim, many of these amazing people also became close friends of mine. The speech therapist, physical therapist, occupational therapist, pulmonary therapist, wheelchair specialist, hospice nurses—the list is long. I warmly connected with each and leaned heavily on their friendships and clinical expertise.

We had help from several of Kim's friends to run errands, help with range of motion exercises, and spend time with Kim. We hired a full-time nurse when the burden became too much for me and some occasional help. Tony Johnson was perfect and a godsend of support until the end.

Kim had hundreds of friends and colleagues. She was dearly loved. Her life group at NewHope Church was a constant source of prayer and support. I also had many friends who desperately wanted to help us. We let them help. That is important. It helped us, but it also helped them. To deny someone the ability to assist does not help them. We created a Meal Train and received hundreds of meals and donations for Grubhub and DoorDash. We enjoyed having dinner with many friends who cooked and delivered the food.

We created a GoFundMe account and received thousands of dollars in donations. An anonymous person donated the use of their beach house in Surf City, North Carolina. Kim's friends from Florida arranged a memorable trip to the mountains near Asheville. Kim and I worked with the ALS Foundation to plan a fundraising walk for ALS and branded the event "Kim Possible and her Posse." A team of Kim's friends was assembled to organize and promote the event.

And we received tremendous support from our pastors at NewHope Church. Dr. Benji Kelley visited our home several times and was open about how "torn up" he was over Kim's diagnosis. He preached a sermon about Kim on Good Friday. We were also very close with Pastor Reece Whitehouse, a spiritual mentor, throughout the ALS journey. Reece also preached a message at NewHope with Kim's story as the centerpiece.

The list could go on and on and on. The support of family, friends, co-workers, neighbors, and random people who heard Kim's story was fantastic. I can't imagine going through such a journey without this huge team of support.

My final comment about caregiving is that the caregiver must find a way to accept and have peace with the diagnosis. In Kim's case, with ALS, we both knew that she would die. We didn't go down the rabbit hole of searching for a cure, questioning the diagnosis, or chasing every crazy idea of how to slow or change the course of the disease. Instead, we agreed to live each day left with joy and gratitude, making the most of each day. I avoided any negative influences on our joy plan. A short visit to an ALS caregiver support group was so full of angry, hurt, and desperately sad people that I did not return. I also minimized time with people who wanted to impress upon me how difficult the coming months or years would be as Kim's disease took hold. I had my hurt, and I knew enough about the darkness of the coming months that other people didn't need to remind me.

Instead, I chose to wake early every morning, watch the beautiful sunrise light up the eastern sky, and then spend my day with my lovely wife, doing what she could do, what we could do, laughing and crying and living the days that were left. This philosophy worked well for me, I think it worked well for Kim, and I'd recommend it for anyone caregiving for another person facing a likely or potentially life-ending disease.

Chapter 9

♡

FAITH

Our second date was at Kim's church. I was already taking my mom to church service on Sunday mornings at the old-fashioned Duke Memorial United Methodist Church in downtown Durham. It was a challenge as Mom struggled to breathe from climbing the few stairs to the main entrance, but she always loved the traditional service once there. After meeting Kim, I started going to church twice on Sundays, just like that old-fashioned expression. First, I took Mom to the Methodist early morning service, and then I would meet Kim at her contemporary church, NewHope, for their second service. I loved the founding pastor, Benji Kelley, and enjoyed the loud and uplifting worship music.

Kim and I would hold hands during the service. It felt so good. I loved falling in love with a woman with the same faith. We discussed God, Jesus, and the differences between Kim's Catholic upbringing and mine in the Christian Church. We prayed together. We sang worship songs during the service. We soon found ourselves volunteering together, first as greeters, then helping with the kindergarten class, and then leading the "New 2 NewHope" program. We participated in two different life groups and then hosted and led a life group at our house. We went on a five-day bus tour of several southern cities with Pastor Benji and two busloads of NewHopers, commemorating the life and works of Dr. Martin Luther King Jr. We both loved how diverse the congregation of NewHope Church was, and we made close friends of folks of all ages, colors, and backgrounds. Being married to a woman with similar spiritual and religious beliefs was a gift. We both enjoyed prioritizing this aspect of our lives and our relationship and committed to growth in our faith.

And then came ALS.

I cannot imagine navigating the trials of ALS without our mutual and deep faith in God. It would have been total hell, I'm sure.

Kim was amazing. Her solid faith in God, and her knowing that she was going to heaven after she died, allowed her to accept and be at peace with the diagnosis quickly. I hope to have that same faith when my number is drawn. As her husband and caregiver, my faith in God and my knowing that Kim would not be suffering after she died sustained me.

Because I was deep in the final stages of my Ph.D. program, with relentless work to be done, I took a break from being part of a life group at church. Kim joined a new group and soon, in typical Kim Blair style, became the leader. Her life group rallied in a big way in supporting her throughout the entire ALS journey. Because of the pandemic, Kim's life group meetings were held on Zoom. Kim always tried to be cheerful and was genuinely interested in the lives of the others. They invited me to several sessions, which was nice. Without stating it, Kim's journey was what every member had on their minds and hearts. You could see it in their eyes. They prayed and prayed and prayed. It was sad watching the despair grow as Kim's condition worsened. People sometimes don't know how to act when they're with someone who is dying. I was learning.

On several occasions, friends and other well-meaning people came to our apartment and later to our new house to pray for Kim. Not only would they pray, but some would place their hands on her and, with loud voices, demand that God hear their cries. They would pray that God would intervene, stop the progression, and bring a cure.

Kim didn't like this. It just made her upset. It made her cry. It made me mad because I saw how it upset Kim. But I kept the anger to myself. Why were these people doing this? I knew that every prayer warrior deeply wanted Kim to be healed. They came to our house with the best of intentions. But Kim had already made peace with the fact that she was going to die. Maybe they didn't know this or didn't want to accept this. And then, maybe, just perhaps, could their prayers work?

Kim told me that she only asked God for a miracle if the miracle could return her to full health—the health she had before ALS. Kim told me that she had no desire to live longer with paralysis, not to mention the inability to speak, eat, or breathe that would come soon.

I never prayed for a miracle. It felt like I would be trying to manipulate God if I did. Who am I to get such a special privilege? Who is Kim to be spared from a disease that kills everyone else it touches? If this disease was part of God's plan, God's plan for Kim, and God's plan for me—for our marriage, then who am I to try to change that?

I did pray. I prayed an intentional prayer. I prayed that Kim stayed close to God, knowing she was going to heaven and would be comfortable and not suffer. I prayed that she would be at peace. I don't know if my prayer was heard, if it was answered, or if it helped. I know that Kim stayed close to God and knew she would be going to heaven. I think she was reasonably comfortable, and I hope that the morphine and other drugs at the end, combined with her private prayers, my prayers, and others' prayers, minimized her suffering. I choose to believe it did.

Kim and I never asked, "Why?" We never got mad at God. I think her faith grew as she came closer to the gates of heaven. I know my faith grew, and for that, I am thankful.

Faith is a mysterious thing. It is uniquely personal. There's always the concern about what other people may think. There's the struggle between different religions, dogmas, and beliefs. The balancing act between "truth and grace." I want to admit that I just don't know, but share what I choose to believe. My beliefs may change over time or stay the same, I don't know.

What will happen to me after I die? I don't know. I'll find out. I choose to believe that I'll go to heaven. I choose to believe that Kim went there after she died. I have no idea if she's still there, if she got reincarnated, if she's an angel hovering around. I feel her presence often, but who knows what that is. I like it, but I don't understand it. I'm OK with the unknowing.

I choose to believe in one loving God, in Jesus Christ, in the Holy Spirit, and that Jesus died for my sins.

My faith is founded on my religious training and understanding of science.

I know that if I take a very powerful microscope and drill down and look closely at anything, like my hand, a rock, or a drop of water, there is nothing. Tangible things, including human bodies, become pure empty space. Energy.

I know that if I take a very powerful telescope and look out into the sky and keep looking further, I never see the end, the wall. There is no end. There is no wall. The universe is infinite and expanding.

Then, what are we? We are empty space. We are energy. We are invisible spiritual beings also mysteriously having, at the same time, a very short physical experience.

God created both—our spiritual essence and our physical selves. Our spirits, unconstrained by time or space, or matter, are intimately connected to God and are with God.

Then we have our human forms, with our five simple and limited senses and human hearts and lungs and brains and miraculously designed healing bodies. Our human forms are bound to this rock called planet Earth by gravity and physicality and human needs for water and food and shelter and love.

Burdened by human thoughts, emotions, desires, and fears, we forget who we are and become separated from our spiritual and eternal nature—from our intimate relationship with God. Our spiritual nature, with God, is infinite and limitless and consists of one emotion—LOVE. I believe this is one of the things that Jesus taught us during his short time here on Earth as a human.

I am a spiritual being having a short physical experience. Kim is also a spiritual being, currently in heaven, who had too short of a physical experience. Kim's biology (her physical body and health) was hacked by ALS, and she soon died.

Kim knew that she was created by God. She knew that God loved her. She loved God. She loved me. She loved other people. Kim taught me the power of true love. Kim taught me that love is the answer.

Kim taught me to live a life of "Born – Love – Die."

From July 5, 2020, Journal

Dear God. Please intervene and make TODAY a good day. Kim is dying. So am I. It is just that our timing is different. Please help me remember that it is a blessing to be so completely in love and to be able (forced) to shift to 100% focus on care for my loved one.

Relax. Release. Accept. Be in spirit mode.

No sense of time, space, stuff.

Just love.

Just presence.

Just peace.

Breath.

One day at a time. One step at a time.

BORN·LOVE·DIE

From Kim's August 28, 2020, Facebook Page:

I read this good reminder this morning. I feel His presence all the time.

"Fear not, for I am with you; be not dismayed, for I am your God; I will strengthen you, I will help you, I will uphold you with my righteous right hand." Isaiah 41:10

Chapter 10

♡

SILENCE

One of the most difficult parts of the ALS journey is losing one's speaking ability. This is horrific for the patient, but it is also one of the worst parts of the disease for the caregiver and other family and friends. At least, it was for me. Some patients with ALS encounter trouble with their throats and voices early on in the journey, and some much later. The disease is unpredictable in how and when the silence will show up, but eventually, it shows up.

Chris Rosati and Don Brown were both able to successfully transition to the use of "speech generation devices" to communicate once they lost their voices. These devices are amazing and allow someone without a voice and without the use of their hands to use their eyes to move a mouse on a screen. These tools can digitally instruct and create words, phrases, gestures, and emotions. Kim and I thought she'd be using a computerized gadget to speak one day, and she even recorded over fifty hours of her voice to be used when that day came. That day never came. Kim tried hard, but it never worked. I don't know if she was too exhausted when her voice disappeared or if she privately chose not to do it. It doesn't matter why. Over her last two months, Kim could not speak at all.

I was angry. I didn't tell Kim but told her speech therapist, Jill. I noticed my anger as Kim failed to learn to use the speech gadget. I had fully expected she'd have no trouble with it. I was counting on it. Several months before, she aced the assessment at the ALS

Clinic and seemed to enjoy playing with the equipment when she had a voice. Now, she had no voice and no success with the machine. My frustration grew to an all-time high as Kim's voice disappeared. Basic communications became a wrestling match.

I told Jill how angry and frustrated I was.

"That's normal," Jill told me as I talked over my cell phone while walking the sidewalks in our new neighborhood.

"Normal?" I exclaimed. "How could this be normal? She did so well in the assessment at the clinic. You were there!" I continued.

"I know," Jill calmly responded. "But this is not unusual. You know how exhausted Kim is. Sometimes an ALS patient has no energy to make it work."

"Then what do I do?" I nearly shouted. "We are almost at a breaking point."

Jill calmly gave me advice. She told me that it was okay that the speech device didn't work and just to put it away in a closet or somewhere to get it away from Kim's sight. Jill suggested that I encourage Kim to speak each syllable very slowly and mentally count with each syllable. She also told me how to print out a chart with letters of the alphabet organized in rows and columns. Jill taught me how to teach Kim to say the row and column of the letter she wanted.

"You're doing a great job, Brett. You should be proud of yourself. I think Kim is as well. This won't be forever," Jill shared as we said goodbye.

I felt better. Jill was becoming more of a therapist for me than a speech therapist for Kim. Her communication advice was great, and both interventions helped for a while.

One afternoon, Kim struggled to tell me that she wanted to send cards to her mom, dad, and two sisters. I found some cute cards on Kim's desk, showed them to her, and she smiled. I sat close to her, looking into her eyes as she struggled to say what she wanted written. Kim did her best to say each syllable slowly. I still couldn't understand some things. I picked up the alphabet chart Jill suggested, and we slowly moved to frustratingly attempt this sad method to complete the card-writing episode.

We did it. The cards were written. Kim seemed pleased. I addressed and stamped the cards and showed them to Kim. She nodded her head, and I took them to the mailbox.

The "speak each syllable" and "alphabet chart" techniques lasted only a few weeks. Then there was complete silence.

Without training, we somehow shifted to Kim using a new way to communicate with me. She would use her eyes.

Blinking once meant "yes."

Blinking twice meant "no."

Staring at something, like the hallway to the bathroom, meant, "I need to go to the bathroom." Or, to the refrigerator, meant, "I need morphine."

And then, there was the worst one. Kim would stare up at the ceiling and hold her gaze there. This always happened after a stressful effort to communicate, to figure out what she was otherwise trying to say. This gesture was Kim's way of saying, to me, "Stop!" Her way of saying, "This conversation is over. Leave me alone."

This happened only a few times. Each time I took it badly. I was tired. I was defensive. It seemed to me that she was saying, "Fuck you." I didn't know how much more I had left.

I would go into another room, find a horizontal line somewhere—the top of a door frame, window frame, top of a computer screen, and say "Born – Live – Die" as I scanned the line. This was my reminder that the suffering Kim and I were experiencing would one day end.

On May 11, 2021, the end happened. Kim quietly went to heaven.

And I'm still here.

I knew Kim very well—maybe better than any other human at the end of her life.

And I know what Kim would say if she could speak. Sharing

what she would say is part of what I shared at her celebration of life, and I feel compelled to share it with you now.

Kim would say, "Don't feel sorry for her." She's in a great place now, and while hanging around here on Earth, she had a great life. It was too short, but she had a great life.

Kim would say, "Live each day fully and do it one day, one moment, at a time. Be all in."

Kim would say, "Don't let worrying about tomorrow ruin your today."

Kim would say, "Born – Love – Die. You're going to die. Everyone you know is going to die. You can't escape that fact. The only question is when, where, and how. But it's going to happen. You don't know how many days you have left. Don't let the fear of death steal the joy of living the life you have right now. And live each day with love."

And Kim would say, "Have fun today. Smile. Laugh. Love each other. Enjoy the magic of this thing called life."

Chapter 11

♡

THE CHOICE

LIFE IS CRUNCHY.
    Life is hard.
    Life is unfair.

But we each have the opportunity, the choice, to decide to flourish between times of crunchy, hard, and unfair events. Make the right choice.

Since Kim died on May 11, 2021, I've followed the same "Born – Love – Die" routine during my morning shower.

This routine sets my philosophy, my framework, my intention for the day. I enter the day with more joy, gratitude, courage, and faith in God.

Since Kim's death, following this daily routine, I've experienced a new level of freedom, power, and magic that I believe are tied to my new level of fearlessness, mindfulness, and intention.

Don't wait until you get a terminal illness and you know you are going to die before you start living.

Wait—you ARE going to die!

You already know that you are going to die.

You have an incurable, terminal condition. We all do. You are going to die. I am going to die. Everyone dies. We just don't know when and where, and how.

Too many people are afraid of death.

Let the awareness of death become your friend, and choose to live each day fully, one day at a time, with joy, with love, and without fear, until death shows up.

This is my plan, and I will forever be thankful to Kim for giving me such a plan. I pray the same for you.

God Bless.

ABOUT THE AUTHOR

Dr. Brett Blair is the founder and president of Best Life Global, LLC. Best Life Global is a high-performance coaching and consulting firm headquartered in Durham, North Carolina. Brett is also the founding partner of Sanford Rose Associates, an executive search firm based in Brighton, Michigan. Brett holds a Ph.D. in Industrial-Organizational Psychology, an MBA-Finance from Tennessee State University, and a BS-Industrial Engineering from the University of Missouri. Brett also studied at Sophia University in Tokyo, Japan. Before founding Best Life Global, Brett enjoyed a 25-year corporate career in international business. Brett's passion is helping people, and he has real-world experience and practical perspectives from which to help professionals in various industries and during all seasons of life. Brett has a unique perspective on personal growth and happiness. He is recognized for his ability to lead others to maximize their potential through living a life of purpose, balance, and significance. He enjoys coaching people through a transformative process of self-discovery, thought observation, and modification of thinking patterns. Brett is a relentless optimist, has strong faith in God, believes that the world is abundant, beautiful, and full of new opportunities and that each day brings the promise of renewal and a new beginning.

Brett has published two books, From *Autopilot to Authentic* and *Living at the Summit*. He can be contacted at bblair@bestlifeglobal.com, and through his website at www.brettblairphd.com.

ACKNOWLEDGMENTS

This book was written with many people's support. The book idea was birthed during the year of ALS, and the year was held together through the help of the people you have already read about and so many more. My family, Kim's family, and our combined sets of friends around the country were the collective support group that held Kim and me up during the year of ALS. You know who you are, and I thank you from the bottom of my heart.

Special thanks go to Dr. Tom Hill for inspiring me to write my first book in 2015, for many years of coaching and mentoring, and for igniting the writer in me. I'm also thankful to my editor, Alice Osborn, and Stacey Blake at Champagne Book Design for the cover art and book formatting.

Thanks to Pastors Benji Kelley and Reece Whitehead for their friendship, encouragement, and spiritual guidance.

Made in United States
North Haven, CT
18 September 2023